Steve

The Happiness Book

Feel Better!

Mike Duffy

The Happiness Book

A Positive Guide To Happiness!

Mike Duffy

I dedicate this book to my beautiful wife, Shannon, my gorgeous daughter, Kendall, and my wonderful son, Mike. I love you with all of my heart and all of my soul. You are my greatest happiness.

ACKNOWLEDGMENTS

I would like to thank many people who have encouraged me over the years. Without your love and support, I wouldn't be nearly as happy as I am today. I would like to thank my father for being such a great man of faith and strength. My mother, for her kindness and tireless devotion. My sisters, Adrienne, Roisin, and Catherine, and their husbands and kids who have given me so much love and laughter. My second mom and dad, Pam and Pat Sullivan, and sister-in-law Erin. My cousin Jimmy and Jane Hardy, James Hardy, Kathryn Hardy, Laura Hardy, Alan and Karen Hardy, Ryan Hardy, and Ross Hardy. Mary and Michael Cleary, Pat and Ken Hardy, and all my Irish family around the world.

My friends: Sean Goode, Kevin and Stephanie Egan, Brian Egan and the Egan clan. Demian Fitzgerald, Chris McCauley, Tag Glynn, Ben Bleichman, Brian Mullaney, Sean Dineen, Doug Covarras, Octavio Jara, Jim and Sara Hickey, Dave Kenada, Josh Sanders, Al Gerona, Gilbert Zucker, Louis Larson, Bill Zurn, Rick DuPont, Ray Montgomery, Dalena Hoang, Francis Chau, George Woo, Tom Waddlington, John McAffee and Kevin Farrell.

My mentors and friends: Alan Olsen, Sarano and Brooke Kelley, Keith Beier, Tom Krumenaker, the BNI Referrals Unlimited team in Redwood City and Phil Goodman.

My board of advisors: Dr. Fred Luskin, Dr. Laura Delizonna, Dr. Prasad Kaipa, Randy Taran and Debbie Gisonni.

All of the inductees of The Happiness Hall Of Fame.

My Kingdom Advisor colleagues including: Rick Hilsbery, Calvin Sid, Carol Hack, Jeff Cave, Barry Tonge, Zanese Duncan, and Ron Blue.

The St. Charles community including: Fr. Dave, Maureen Grazioli, the fantastic faculty of St. Charles school, Ernie Von Emster, Dennis and Tanya O'Malley, Fred Buecher, Matt Earnshaw, Ben Glenn, Bob Stafford, and the St. Charles' Men's Club.

The Archbishop Molloy family including: Br. Leo, Br. Milke, Br. Hogan, Br. Declan, Ted McGuinness, Carl Ahlgren, Kevin Brandon, Jim McNulty, and Larry O'Brien.

My wonderful editor, Stephanie Marohn.

CONTENTS

PART II

Take Action!

ABOUT THE AUTHOR

Mike Duffy is the founder of Happiness Publishing, LLC. He has been researching happiness for over 30 years. He is friends with and has interviewed the brightest minds in the field of positive psychology. He is the author of *The Happiness Book For Men*, *The Happiness Book For Kids: A Child's Guide To Happiness! Volume I & II* and *The Happiness Book For Little Christians: A Biblical Guide To Happiness!* Mike was a professional stand-up comedian. He has performed at the top clubs and even was an MC at Woodstock 94'. He has appeared in a Facebook commercial. Mike loves to speak about how you can gain greater happiness and joy in your wonderful and precious life. He combines humor and the latest happiness research to entertain audiences. His audiences include corporations, universities and organizations. Mike is the founder of The Happiness Hall Of Fame. The Happiness Hall Of Fame recognizes, encourages and celebrates people and organizations that make other people happy. The website is www.happinesshalloffame.com

WHAT THIS BOOK CAN DO FOR YOU

Why do some people succeed and other people meander through life going from one failure to another? The American Heritage Dictionary defines success as "The achievement of something desired, planned, or attempted." I believe the biggest reason for the difference in outcomes is that successful people are laser-focused and accountable to their goals. To achieve your goals, you need to set them in stone. Then you have to have a plan. Success is a slow, purposeful, dedicated process and not an event. This book will deal with two important components of success: health and happiness. You will laugh as you learn!

Throughout my life, everyone has told me that I am one of the happiest people they know. I love to make people laugh and feel good. I was a professional stand-up comedian in New York City. I have worked with some of the most famous comedians at the Comic Strip Live!, Caroline's on Broadway, and many other venues. I was an emcee at Woodstock '94. Laughter is an essential part of a happy life.

I have been obsessed with the human emotion of happiness and how to increase it since I was seventeen years old. That was the year I lost my mother to cancer. I needed to find the secrets to happiness to get over the loss. I have read more than a hundred books on happiness and self-improvement. I have attended countless seminars, workshops, and classes, read hundreds of research papers, watched all of the shows, listened to most of the CDs and tapes on the subject of happiness. I earned a degree in psychology because I wanted to unlock the secrets of the human mind.

The first section of this book covers how you can achieve more happiness, have better relationships, enjoy work more, and have an incredible, joyful life. Here I break down the science and principles of happiness that I learned from all my study. As an example, the Grant study, which started in 1938, followed 268 male Harvard undergraduates throughout their lives. The purpose of the study was to determine which factors contribute to success and human flourishing. President John F. Kennedy was one of the study participants. Psychiatrist George Vaillant directed the study for more than thirty years. In the article "What Makes Us Happy?" by Joshua Wolf Shenk, published in the *Atlantic* in 2009, Vaillant states, "Happiness is love. Full stop."

The second part of this book helps you take action on your goals. Please do yourself a favor and act on your dreams. With a deadline, dreams become goals. I wish you all the best in becoming the person that you were meant to be! You can do this!

If I were to sum up in one word what this book is all about, it is about love. That is my message. Love yourself and those around you. If you love other people, you will be rewarded with abundant amounts of love and blessings in return. When the love that you send out is being returned to you, you will know true happiness. Love is, always was, and always will be the answer to the question, "Why are we here?" We are here to love.

PART I

HOW TO BE HAPPY

CHAPTER 1

HAPPINESS IS A CHOICE

*Folks make up their mind to choose to be
as happy as they choose to be.*
—ABRAHAM LINCOLN

*Happiness is the meaning and the purpose of life,
the whole aim and end of human existence.*
—ARISTOTLE

Joke: An elderly couple is in marriage therapy. The therapist asks the wife, "In the morning do you wake up grumpy?" She looks at her husband and says, "No, I let him sleep!"

Happiness is a positive and joyful state of mind. *The Merriam-Webster Dictionary* defines happiness as "a state of well-being and contentment or a pleasurable or satisfying experience." Remember, no one can make you happy except yourself.

Here are some advantages of being happy:

- **Increased productivity.** Ever try to accomplish something when you are depressed? You simply don't care about the task at hand. You are more effective when you are in a happy state of mind.

- **More friends.** People like associating with other people that bring them up and make them laugh. I believe that friends are one of life's true blessings. Friends are like compound interest. The more friends you have, the more new people you are introduced to. The more people you are introduced to, the more friends you will have. And on and on...
- **Better health.** Research has shown that people that have a positive attitude are healthier than pessimistic people. Depressed people have higher incidences of illness.
- **Make more money.** Customers want to work with happy service providers. Management wants to promote effective, positive people that are not complaining to them day after day. Where productivity lives, raises and bonuses follow.
- **Reduced stress.** People that are in a happy state are less likely to report feelings of stress. Stress can lead to high blood pressure and cancer. Stay happy and you'll stay healthy.
- **Improved work environment.** Happiness in an office is contagious. In Silicon Valley where I work, many companies focus on making their employees happy. At some companies, they have fantastic free food. I've been to some of them. The food is awesome *and* healthy! Some have free haircuts, oil changes, and dry cleaning. Why? It is because happy employees do better work and do not leave as frequently.
- **Better relationships.** Being in love with a happy person is so much more fulfilling than having a relationship with a complainer. A happy partner will look for the good in you. They are up for new experiences. They want to make great new memories. They want to squeeze as much out of life with their loved one before time runs out. Why would someone leave a partner that makes him or her happy?

- **Happier children.** Kids mimic what their parents do. If you are an alcoholic, it increases the chance that your kids will be too. Be a happyholic! Show them your resilience to life's problems, that you don't let the problems get you down. Teach them your strategies for getting over life's hurdles with a smile. Make your home a sanctuary where love, laughter, and creativity thrive. Your children will get better grades, better jobs, and better lives as a result of your positive influence.

Dale Carnegie said, "Success is getting what you want. Happiness is wanting what you get." What is it that you want? What are you willing to do to get it? You must realize that whatever it is that you want to achieve comes with a cost. It comes with action and modification of your behavior. Are you willing to get to work early and stay late in order to be wealthy? Are you willing to stop saying bad things to yourself and be happy?

Choose to ignore bad things that happened in your past. Larry Ellison was given up for adoption when he was nine months old. He didn't meet his biological mother until he was forty-eight years old. Strike one. He never got a college degree. Strike two. He was briefly the richest man in the world in the year 2000. Home run.

Larry Ellison once said, "I have had all of the disadvantages required for success." That is a great way to think about one's misfortune. Instead of comparing your life to others' great advantages, realize that great men and women have often come from obscurity. You can use it as a great driver to propel your life forward. Success doesn't necessarily bring happiness, but success can help you bless others, which can lead to happiness. Larry Ellison has helped many people with his hard work. Kevin, my best man at my wedding and the godfather to my daughter, got his first job out of college at

Oracle. It was on the help desk. It was a thankless, low-paying position. But this first job, helped Kevin propel himself to the top of Silicon Valley.

For those of you that are getting push-back from people that want to pigeonhole you into what you have done previously, take heed of Larry Ellison's words. He said, "When you innovate, you've got to be prepared for everyone telling you you're nuts." Don't be afraid to take your career or entrepreneurship to the next level. The critics will have a hard time accepting your rise. That's their problem. Do not accept their negative criticism. Some will just not get what you are trying to do or become. Most people mean no harm; they have just not seen someone want to rise out of mediocrity. Some are jealous and want to harm. Regardless of their intentions, grab hold of that ladder and start climbing. Keep your happiness with you as you ascend. You will face bumps, bruises, and other battle scars that other successful people have endured before you. They are badges of courage. They are signs of happiness. Make sure you treat people well along the way.

A lot of people dream about winning the lottery. That's when they think happiness will come pouring in like a flood. Some lottery winners wish they'd never won. Sometimes the money that they dreamed of destroys them. Studies have shown that there is a happiness plateau at $75,000 a year in income. There is no great increase in happiness between someone making $75,000 a year and someone making $7,500,000 a year in income. Once your basic human needs have been met, you are no different than a Rockefeller when it comes to happiness. We all still want to be loved and respected. Money cannot buy either.

George Bernard Shaw said, "People are always blaming their circumstances for what they are. I don't believe in circumstances. The people who get on in this world are the people who get up and look for the circumstances they want, and if they can't find them, they make them." Make your own circumstances. A lot of people rest on excuses. They waste their life blaming others instead of getting out there and grabbing that brass ring. Throughout this book, I highlight people that had adverse situations but rose above. Be like these people.

Take the limits off your life. You can achieve anything you set your mind to. Raise your level of expectancy. I encourage you to notice just how good you have it. If you are reading this, you are literate. If you are listening to this book, you have hearing. As you become grateful for even the little things, you will become happier. The more you become thankful for what you have, you will compound your joy, like a snowball gathering more snow as it rolls down a hill.

Look around you right now. Everything you see was once an idea that became a decision. Nothing can be built or created without it being thought up first. All you need to change your life for the better are better thoughts and action. Positive thoughts and thoughts of achievement are the building blocks of your new life.

What is it you want to be? Who is it you want to become? If you want to become an author, put down this book and start writing now. If you want to be a teacher, go back to school at night and on the weekends. If you want a job that is not in your area, move. You need to attach action to your great thoughts and plans.

What is holding you back? How can you overcome that obstacle? Sit down and write a list. Or, better yet, put it in your smartphone, that way, you can add new goals and delete achieved goals with time. Your smartphone is always with you. There is no excuse. I have an iPhone. It has a notes app. On it, I have a long list of things I want to accomplish. I show the list to people. I'm sure you have had triumphs in the past. You should strive to create new ones again and again. Take a picture when you hit these milestones and keep them in a file marked "Victories." It will always bring a smile to your face. You can show them to your family. It will encourage them and you to begin new journeys, develop new talents, and be braver.

Choose to live in an attitude of gratitude. I was driving to work one day and I thought, "I'm forty-five. I'm a middle-aged man!" The thought that I was middle-aged had never crossed my mind before. Instead of thinking that my life was half over, I immediately thought of all the blessings that I have in my life: a great career, a great family, and wonderful friends. My next thought was "I wish I was middle-aged ten years ago!"

By being grateful for just being alive, you can accept that life comes with problems. Everybody has problems. Dr. Norman Vincent Peale said, "The only people without problems are in the cemetery." You are not in the cemetery yet. While you have this precious above-ground time, make the most of it! Don't let worry or anxiety cut into your happy time. Shake off your negative emotions. Tell your bad thoughts when they rush into your mind, "I don't have a lot of time. I'm not going to let you take what little I've got."

Dr. Peale also said, "Change your thoughts and you change your world." Imagine you were a mayfly. A mayfly has about twenty-four hours to live. Would you be a mayfly that uses those twenty-four hours sitting on a park bench crying about what little time you have left? Or would you be the mayfly that makes the most of the precious twenty-four hours? We are all mayflies, some with more time than others. Just because you get diagnosed with a terminal illness and have six months to live, doesn't mean a bus can't hit you after leaving the doctor's office. Just because your doctor gives you a clean bill of health doesn't mean you can't die changing a light bulb. Change your thoughts. Be grateful.

Your emotions dictate whether you are happy or not. Money, fame, being in a relationship, or having a great job does not. If you want to be happy, change your emotions. How do you change your emotions? Ask yourself questions like: "Will this current situation matter four years from now? What is actually funny about what's going on right now?" By inserting laughter into the current situation, you will laugh and be happy. You cannot be sad and laugh at the same time. Laughter changes emotions instantly. That's why I love to think about funny things that have happened to me or funny movie lines that I have seen. I always try to shift conversations to funny subjects because that's where I love to live: in laughter land. It's a wonderful place that costs nothing to visit. You can leave whenever you want and everybody has a great time during their stay. The best part of laughter land is everyone that enters is happy, even on a short visit.

Be proactive about happiness. Most people are passive about happiness. They are waiting for it to chase them down and tackle them. I knew full well that I would never meet my wife sitting in my condo in Pacific Heights in San Francisco, watching TV. I was under no delusion that a beautiful, intelligent, and caring woman was going to fall through the ceiling and onto my lap. I went out and met as many women as I could. I placed myself in many uncomfortable and awkward situations because I knew I was reaching for my dream of a great wife. My dream came true. You must proactively seek happiness both internally, via positive thoughts and meditation, and externally, through interactions with the environment and great people. Build positive relationships and stretch yourself for the greater good. You'll be very glad you did!

Happiness is a discipline. Just as you wouldn't let a stranger come into your house and take your dinner every night, you cannot let people steal your happiness. And believe me, they will try.

The funniest man I ever knew was a man named Mickey Stapleton. He was one of my father's friends from Dublin, Ireland. He was the Irish Johnny Carson. Everybody loved Mickey. His nickname was Mickey White Shoes. He frequently wore terrible white shoes because men's white shoes are preposterous. You cannot be cool sporting white shoes. He loved when people would make fun of his shoes because that meant he could make fun of himself. He always had a parade of nonstop jokes at the ready. Even his bad jokes were funny. I never once had a serious conversation with him. I never heard him have a serious conversation. I said that to him once and he said, "Why should I be so serious? You see, when God was making me, he asked me what kind of nose I wanted. I thought he asked what kind of rose I wanted and I said I wanted a big red one!"

During a burial at a gravesite, the casket of one of our family friends was being lowered into the ground. The priest was standing at the head of the hole. The ground gave way and the priest fell into the grave. The widow screamed in dire fright. Mickey looked down into the grave and said, "Father, can you please stop your fooling around and come up out of that hole. We are trying to have a respectable funeral here!" Everybody broke their heart laughing, including the widow who had been at her wits' end just moments before. Everybody laughed for ten minutes and, to this day, the widow thinks back to one of her worst days and tells the story to others with a smile and a laugh.

Mickey died of lung cancer in 2010. He was an incredible joy to know. Have you ever heard someone use the put-down line, "He thinks he's God's gift to the world?" Mickey *was* God's gift to the world. He celebrated every moment of his existence. He was one of the happiest people in the world. He never became wealthy. He never had a prestigious job. He was a painter in a city hospital.

All of the doctors and nurses would flock to him to have him lift their spirits on tough days. They would sometimes send him (the hospital painter) in to a family that just got news their child was dying or other similar tragedies. He would help the family get through one of the most difficult moments a human can ever endure. He would always leave a room with the sound of laughter behind him. He was a true angel that walked the earth and I miss him very much. I'm grateful that I got a chance to know him. I'm also grateful that I told him how much I loved him and his joie de vivre. To which he smiled slyly and replied, "Is 'joie de vivre' white shoes in French?!"

CHAPTER 2

KEEP LEARNING

An investment in knowledge pays the best interest.
—Benjamin Franklin

Zig Ziglar was one of the greatest motivational speakers of all time. His homespun wit and wisdom made him a sought after speaker all around the world. He came up with a way that the average person could increase their knowledge. He called it "Automobile University." He added up all the hours the average person spent in their car and recommended that people listen to books on tape and learn while driving. With smartphones today, there is no reason why you can't download knowledge apps and learn while you drive. If you don't have a smartphone, go to the library and take out CDs of topics that interest you.

Improving yourself constantly will make you more valuable to an employer and a more interesting friend and spouse, and keep you sharper. Turn off the TV and read or listen to a book on tape. Go to a lecture. You don't need to watch *Friends* or *Seinfeld* for the thirty-second time.

I hadn't been to college in two decades and my firm sent me to Harvard for an intensive workshop on topics ranging from astrophysics to American literature. We had six courses with six different top Harvard professors. They were all incredible. While they were teaching, they were laughing frequently and telling funny anecdotes. They really enjoyed what they did for a living and it showed. Their enthusiasm for their subjects was evident. They had found what made them happy and they got to share it with the world. You could tell that they would do it for free, if they had to. It got me excited about education and the enjoyment that can result.

On the second night of the Harvard program, I met my Boston friends at a Boylston Street restaurant. My friend Chris asked me how the program was going. I said, "I'm high right now!" Chris asked me "What do you mean, you're high right now?" I said, "The professors got me high!" He said, "The professors slipped you drugs?" I said, "No, they were so good at teaching and they had so much knowledge about the subject, it got me in such a good mood, it got me high!" The professors' enthusiasm inspired me to spend more time reading about and researching happiness.

Continuing education is very important. If you're stuck in a dead-end job because you don't have your degree, see if your company will pay for your education. A lot of companies will do this. You can go to school at night and on the weekends. You can also get a degree online. If you can't afford college, consider changing jobs and moving to a company that does provide for education. There is no reason why you can't get a college degree if you really want one.

If you already have a degree, audit classes at a local college. Pick your favorite subject and just go. You don't even have to take the tests. You don't get a grade. You can just learn more about a subject that interests you. It is so much better than watching the local bad news every night. You will be around other people interested in the same subject as you. You can make new friends and discuss things that matter to you. It's so refreshing to pick the brain of someone on the same wavelength. It also gets you out of the house and moving. Studies have shown that people who stimulate their brain have less risk of Alzheimer's and other diseases of aging.

I have taken a number of continuing education courses at Stanford University. The teachers are fantastic! I get so happy whenever I am on Stanford campus. There is a feeling of vibrance and energy unlike any other place. I have taken courses on happiness, public speaking, film editing and failure. Yes, they have a class on failure. Failure is a necessary step on the path to success.

Dr. John Krumboltz, the author of *Fail Fast Fail Often* had us form a group of three students. Every week we had to pledge to do something we had always wanted to do. We were accountable to each other. My first task was to interview him. I thoroughly enjoyed my time in discussion of life's deeper meanings and glorious subtleties with him. He has been teaching at Stanford for over 55 years!

You can even watch college courses for free at www.coursera. org. You can watch great professors from Stanford, Princeton, Duke, and Georgia Tech. I went to Georgia Tech my freshman year of college. I was an electrical engineering student. Trust me, it's a great school. The last time I checked, you can choose from the following course topics and more: biology and life sciences, computer science, mathematics, education, medicine, humanities and social sciences, and business and management. How can you go wrong with free education?

CHAPTER 3

UP CYCLES AND DOWN CYCLES

*The game has its ups and downs, but you can never
lose focus of your individual goals and you can't
let yourself be beat because of lack of effort.*
—MICHAEL JORDAN

I define an Up Cycle as a positive state of being that is initiated by a good behavior. An example would be starting a diet or an exercise regimen. Spending more time with your children instead of watching TV can start it. As humans, we are preprogrammed to become happy as a result of our hard work. Look at the face of a child when you praise them for drawing a picture of you. The smile goes from ear to ear. Look at pictures of people standing next to their new car they worked so hard to get. The elation jumps right off the page. When people get promotions, they fist-pump, smile, and tell everyone they know. When I became a senior vice president at my firm, I was happy for months. I'm still happy! I started out as a sales assistant, answering phones, executing trades on paper tick-ets, and recording each stock purchase and sale manually with a pen in my boss's book every morning. Sometimes it took hours to painstakingly and precisely write all the trades down. Mistakes were not allowed. For that reason alone, I have been in a work Up Cycle all these years.

Travel is a great way to start an Up Cycle. It will open your mind to all the possibilities that can occur if you apply yourself. It is a great way to see all the great creations that humans have made over the centuries. Visit places you are interested in and where you've always wanted to go.

Plan your trip before you leave. That way you have a schedule and are not just sitting in your hotel room wondering what to do. Like anything in life, ask people who have already been to the place for tips. Buy a book on the place you're going to visit. Go online and see reviews of the hotel where you're going to stay. Call a travel agent. Yes, a travel agent! They still exist. They may actually be able to beat the price that you found online. They may have already been to the place or have sent lots of clients there. They will have feedback from their clients and be a great resource for you.

Ask your friends on Facebook and other social networking sites if anyone's ever gone to your chosen destination. Have them send you photos and give you recommendations on where to go. Go to travel sites like Trip Advisor to get advice from people that have been there as well. Google videos of the place you want to visit.

Up Cycles are always started by a conscious decision to improve. They are continued by the same desire to be better than the day before. Examine what you want out of life and start an Up Cycle. You'll be glad you did.

I define a Down Cycle as a negative state of being that is initiated by a bad behavior, such as overeating or being sedentary. Cheating on your spouse can start it. Ignoring your children can start it. It is a bad seed planted by you that only grows worse and worse and bears toxic and poisonous fruit.

Sometimes people do or say horrible things to us. We cannot control that. All we can control is what we do in our own lives. Shake it off and start an Up Cycle for yourself. When you make progress on a goal, you feel empowered. Lose your job? Go out and find a better one. Did your spouse or your loved one leave you for another? Find someone that will treat you the way you should be treated. This is your *opportunity* to find your soul mate. See what I did there? I took one of the most soul-crushing, depressing times in one's life and changed perspective. See things always as an opportunity to upgrade, to advance, to grow, and to prosper.

I am a huge fan of underdogs. My favorite cartoon as a kid was *Underdog.* I have always had to overcome obstacles to succeed. I have highlighted three of my favorite football underdogs in this book. They all have had to overcome obstacles to get to success. They have all had ups and downs. They have had Up Cycles and Down Cycles. They are known, however, for not giving up and being bold in the face of adversity.

In 2010, the NFL channel named Kurt Warner the greatest undrafted free agent. He went from being released from the Green Bay Packers in training camp and bagging groceries at the Hy-Vee grocery store in 1994 to Super Bowl MVP in 2000. How did he do that?

Kurt Warner dreamed of being an NFL quarterback. His dream was not to be a grocery bagger. In life, you must sometimes start at the bottom. No NFL team wanted him. Nobody believed in him except himself. So he decided to start an Up Cycle and gain the skills and knowledge of professional football in the Arena Football League. He worked extremely hard at his craft. He devoted himself to being the best Arena Football League quarterback. This dedication brought his team, the Iowa barnstormers, to two Arena Bowl appearances.

This success helped him get signed by the St. Louis Rams. They shipped him off to NFL Europe. Instead of starting a Down Cycle, he grabbed this chance and led the league in passing yards and touchdowns. The Rams brought him back to the United States. They promoted him to second string behind Trent Green. Trent Green tore his ACL (anterior cruciate ligament; in the knee) in a preseason game. Always prepare yourself for greatness. You never know when it will come calling.

Kurt Warner was well prepared. The Arena league specialized in high-octane offense. A quarterback needed to get the ball out fast and be accurate. Because of his training, he starred in what was nicknamed "the Greatest Show on Turf." This unknown former grocery bagger ended up on the cover of *Sports Illustrated* midway through the 1999 season with the caption "Who *Is* This Guy?" He threw for over 4,300 yards and forty-one touchdowns. His completion percentage was over 65 percent. By starting at the bottom, he had one of the top seasons a quarterback has ever had. He took a team that had won nine games the last two seasons combined and brought them to Super Bowl XXXIV. With the game tied and two minutes to play, he drove the Rams seventy-eight yards and threw a touchdown to Isaac Bruce to win the game. He was named league MVP and Super Bowl MVP. Not bad for a Hy-Vee bagger nobody believed in.

Injuries played a major role in Kurt Warner's career after the 1999 season. He never let them stop him, however. In 2001, he brought the Rams back to the Super Bowl. They lost. He did not turn to drugs and alcohol, which would have started a Down Cycle. He kept working.

The Rams got rid of him and he went to the New York Giants. The kid with the pedigree, Payton Manning's brother, Eli Manning, replaced him. He did not get depressed and choose infidelity, which would have started a Down Cycle. He kept on working, training, sacrificing, and getting better. This man had no quit in him. The writing was on the wall that the Giants wanted Eli. He did not want to sit and watch someone else work while getting paid. He went to the Arizona Cardinals in 2005.

At the Cardinals, he was injured again and was replaced as the starter by Josh McCown. He kept rehabbing and working hard, believing that if he kept on going, he would eventually succeed. In 2006, he was replaced again, by the hot new thing, quarterback Matt Leinart. He never gave up and hung in there, seeing action when Leinart went down, over the next two seasons.

In 2008, new coach Ken Wisenhunt named Warner the starter. Because Warner never gave in to other people's lack of confidence in him, he was ready. He delivered big time. He took the Cardinals to the Super Bowl at the age of thirty-six. The team lost. It wasn't for his lack of trying to win the game. Kurt Warner has the record for the most yards passing in each of his three Super Bowl appearances.

He retired from football on January 29, 2010. During his up-and-down career, he came to own over twenty-six NFL quarterback records. He could have played another year. He wanted to have more time to spend with his wife and seven children. He was given the NFL Walter Payton Man of the Year award in 2008. This is an award that is given to players of the highest moral character. In 2009, he won a poll by the readers of *Sports Illustrated* for best role model on and off the field. He is the recipient of the Bart Starr Award. It is given to people that exhibit outstanding character. Bart Starr himself said, "We have never given this award to anyone who is more deserving."

In life there are many people to emulate. Choose carefully. Don't fall into the trap of emulating "bad boys" or other such dimwits. Study the underdogs who show perseverance in the face of outrageous odds. Model their propensity to climb out of bad situations and achieve victory. Always try to be in an Up Cycle.

CHAPTER 4

LONELINESS IS THE ENEMY OF HAPPINESS

*Loneliness and the feeling of being
unwanted is the most terrible poverty.*
—MOTHER TERESA

Do not be lonely. Loneliness is a choice. If you are lonely right now, join something. If you wish you had more friends, get involved with an organization, a cause, a faith-based group, or an animal shelter. Whatever interests you have, there is an organization for it. When you find that group, ask the people you like out to coffee. When you figure out if you would like to have that person as a friend, have dinner with them. Add them to your Facebook friends. Dr. Wayne Dyer, PhD, once said, "Friends are God's apology for your family."

You can never have enough friends. Make enough friends so you never have to sit alone at home if you don't want to. If you work in an office, start a monthly "Meeting of the Minds." Everyone gets together at a local bar for a drink. My dad always said, "If you want to get to know a person, have a drink with them." There is a world of happiness and friendship waiting for you. You have to take the first step.

I was born in 1967. I am one of the last generations to know social society and how it worked before the Internet. I am a big proponent of technology and the Internet. I have also seen how the Internet can lead to isolation and loneliness. Interacting with your friends outside of Facebook is a lot more important than having virtual relationships online. You can fall into a pattern that you are keeping up with your friends online but never see them. Instead you spend your nights at home, with your computer on your lap while you watch TV alone. Real friendships need face-to-face interaction. They need to be strengthened by creating memories, building trust, and helping each other out. An e-mail can only go so far. Years go by and the friendship never grows.

Being online exposes you to horrifically bad and depressing news from all around the world. You do not need to feed your soul all of this bad news. It leads to unproductive worry and depression. My favorite uncle, Ken, gave up reading the newspaper when he was forty. He called it the "Bad news–paper." He wouldn't let it destroy his "'appiness." He was a wonderful, colorful cockney from London. Part artful dodger, part Santa Claus, he had a heart for children.

He would visit us in New York City, twice a year. We would be so excited to hear that he was coming because he always took an interest in my three sisters and me. He would get off the plane from London, come to our house, and take us straight to the candy store. Jet lag and adults be darned. He did not waste time watching on the local TV news who got shot. Instead, he included us in conversations and played games with us. We only understood half of what he said; his cockney accent was so thick. No matter what he said, it always sounded like "Pip pip! Cheerio, dah-ling!" He was in the British army when he was younger. He had a long career at British Airways. He reminded me of Dick Van Dyke's father, Grandpa Potts, in the movie *Chitty Chitty Bang Bang*.

After he retired, he got a job as a janitor at a local school in Devon, which is in the English countryside. He loved to mentor children. One of the boys he mentored became a top surgeon in England. When he received news that my uncle Ken had a few days to live, he dropped everything and stayed by his side, holding his hand until he passed. My uncle had changed his life. A janitor with very little schooling had inspired a lost boy who had nobody that believed in him. Uncle Ken had spent time with a child that nobody wanted to play with, talk to, or deem important at all. Ken taught the unwanted boy that he could do anything with his life, if he applied himself. He made him laugh with old jokes and brightened his spirit with hard candy that he always had in his pockets. This elite surgeon saved countless lives and helped people live free from pain and misery. He said, without my uncle Ken, he would never have had the belief that he could do something positive for others.

Like a stone thrown into a pond, your kindness can have a ripple effect outward on the lives of so many people. Who will be there when you die? What will your legacy be? Who will you inspire?

Instead of wasting your time reading the bad news, why don't you make good news? Why don't you be in the newspaper doing something great for your community or something great for your business. It's free advertising. Wouldn't you love to read something positive about yourself in print? Wouldn't you like your friends, neighbors, enemies, and potential future employers or customers reading about how great you are? Everyday, newspapers have space to fill. Why not let them tell your wonderful new story.

I'm not saying don't have a knowledge about what's going on in the world. But if you are going to read the news, read the business section. If you're going to watch the news, watch business news. There are often interviews with the top thought leaders on market trends. Those are things that you *need* to know.

You are at your peak performance when you are happy and positive. We have a very limited time on this earth; make the absolute most of it. You need to have discipline over what you read, what you speak, and what you expose your mind to. You owe it to those you love to be positive. Positivism is infectious. You will send out ripples of happiness and lift people out of sadness with your positivism.

Lead by example, especially if you are a parent. Talk is cheap. Decide right now that you will be happy and adopt a resolve of steel to follow through with it, regardless of the situation you find yourself in. What is the result of this decision? Many results! First, you will be happy! Second, people will seek your company. Third, your business will succeed. People are naturally attracted to happy people. They want to do business with happy people.

If you are not currently happy, tell yourself you are. Say to yourself, "I am happy. I am positive. I am successful." This can be your mantra. You have to be your biggest fan. You have to be your biggest believer. When someone asks you how you are doing, you tell them, "I am doing great!" My favorite thing to say is "Life just keeps getting sweeter every day!" I could have my left foot in an alligator's mouth and my right foot in a bear trap and if someone asked me, "How are you doing?" my response would not change. I would still say, "I am doing fantastic!" Why? Life is too short and too precious to succumb to negative thinking. I live in an attitude of gratitude. If I am alive, I am happy.

An attitude of gratitude means being grateful for everything that comes your way. I am old enough now to look back on my life and see that all the bad things that happened to me were for a purpose. My mother died when I was seventeen years old. She was only forty-nine years old. That taught me that life is short. It must be seized, enjoyed, and attacked.

During college, I lost a job as a waiter because a customer complained that the food took too long to come out. It wasn't my fault. All but one of the cooks had called in sick and the restaurant was packed. I was devastated. I had never been fired before. It wasn't fair.

My next job was as a sales assistant at Paine Webber. It launched my career. Today I could kiss that wonderful, complaining customer. Willie Jolley coined a great phrase, "Your setback is just a setup for your comeback." It is so true. Look back on your life. You've had times when a door closed and, because of that abrupt and often painful occurrence, another door opened. A relationship ended that broke your heart. You found someone else that was better suited to you. Someone outbid you on that house you wanted so bad. A different and better house came on the market, which you bought. The neighbor's child at the new house became your child's lifelong best friend. Always find the silver lining. Throw your stone into the pond of only good people. You will be surprised at the number of fantastic friendships that come from the ripples.

CHAPTER 5

HOW TO BE HAPPY AT WORK

You do your best work if you do a job that makes you happy.
—BOB ROSS

I truly believe that I can overcome any obstacle. Whenever there is a "wall" in front of me, I will go over it, go under it, go around it, or smash right through it. When that doesn't work, I will simply out-wait it. I have had nightmare bosses at jobs where I simply decided I would wait until the boss got fired, got promoted, or quit. My goal was to outlast them. I knew I needed to be where I was. I loved my job and I liked the company; I just didn't like the manager.

Managers are usually on a carousel. If you don't like yours today, just wait and there will be a new one soon enough. Until then, work even harder, keep your smile on, and refuse to let them steal your joy. Of course, this is only if you want to stay at your company and you see potential for promotion. Otherwise, you should leave. Your happiness isn't worth staying at a job you hate. There are always op-tions. If you have to move, then move. I moved all the way across the country to San Francisco at age twenty-seven. I left behind all of my wonderful New York friends and dear family. I knew nobody in San Francisco. I had only $7,000 to my name, no car, no network, no friends, and no place to live. It was the greatest decision I ever made.

It's okay to start at the bottom. Just make sure you work yourself up. I have switched companies because of greater opportunity. Never be afraid to leave your company if you get a better offer. Weigh your decisions carefully and ask to speak to people at your potential new company. Each time I have left a company, it has worked out for the better. Some companies don't promote from within. You have to leave if you want to take the next step up the ladder. Take it. You can handle the extra responsibility. You have the wherewithal to handle every situation. You are not the only person to step off the cliff and jump to a higher rung of the ladder. If you fall off, try again. Thomas Edison failed miserably for years trying to invent the light bulb. You will have learned from your mistakes too. Wisdom comes from failure. Happiness comes from progress.

Try to make your manager your friend. Take them out to lunch and pay for it. Be a productive partner to your manager. When you approach them with a problem, don't say, "This stinks or I hate this." You should say, "There is a problem with ___. I need your help to come up with a solution. So far my most constructive solution to this problem is ___." Always try to come up with a constructive way to fix a problem.

Don't jump from job to job because you don't get along with your manager. You could leave your current job, work for the dream manager that hired you, and attend their farewell party three days later. At the farewell party, your new nightmare manager hands you your new weekend productivity schedule. Managers get fired, leave the company, get promoted, move to new departments, go on sick leave, and even die. It is up to you to try to get along with every manager you work with. You could also become a manager.

It is a hard job being a manager. You have to say no when you want to say yes. For you managers out there reading this, be honest with your employees. If you have to implement a new mandate that you don't agree with, level with your employees. Tell them that if it were up to you, you wouldn't be doing this, but upper management has this vision, which we all have to implement at this time. This will show your employees that you are on their side. They will respect you for it and work harder to get the new program achieved. With you on their side, they will view you as one of them. Have an ironic prize like a Hula-Hoop for the employee who jumped through hoops to tackle this inane mandate. It will lighten the mood and make everyone laugh. Laughter is the road to and the destination of happiness.

As an employee, try to be a bridge between management and the workforce. Take on tasks with enthusiasm. Be an example for the other employees. The universe does not owe you a living. You are lucky to have this opportunity to shine. Make the most of it. Use it as a stepping-stone to something greater. Brighten the lives of everyone around you. When I come into work every day, I say hello to everyone like I just won the lottery. I mean everyone. There is no one that does not deserve a big, warm hello in the morning.

Be grateful that you have a job! Employment provides self-esteem. Some people's philosophy of how to get ahead at work is the squeaky-wheel strategy. The squeaky wheel gets the grease. They will complain, annoy, and overload management until they get their way. I don't want to be a squeaky wheel. I don't want to be that cranky person at work who gets things because they are perpetually in a bad mood and are given things to shut up. They may get things in the short term, but they are burning bridges.

In Silicon Valley and other communities, people will move to new companies in teams. They leave behind the squeaky wheels and form newer, better companies. Throughout your career, you will create a reputation. Believe it or not, you are a brand. You have to build a sterling brand that will be attractive to future employers or customers. Do you want to be known as a valuable person that will enrich your employers or a toxic, lazy person that has a bad reputation? The choice is yours.

Here are some other ways to increase your happiness at work:

- **Forgive yourself when you make a mistake at work.** Own up to it and quickly come up with a solution. Few people own up to mistakes these days. Your peers and manager will respect you more if you do.

- **Celebrate coworkers' successes.** Don't be jealous if someone beside you gets a promotion. Understand that it's a good thing if success is going on around you. It means that you can create success one day too. Also, people will make you feel special when you get promoted.

- **Change your perspective.** If you work in customer service, don't see yourself as the person who gets beat up all day long by customers' problems. See yourself as one of the most important members of the corporate team. Without people like you, the company would lose its existing customers and its reputation. One of the reasons Apple and Ritz Carlton are so successful is because of their customer service.

- **Be happy right now!** Don't wait until you get a raise or a promotion to be happy. A raise will make you happy for a short time, but that will fade. Then what? Be happy today.

- **Don't be afraid to ask.** You will have questions about your job. The best employees are not fearful to ask someone when they need help. Your biggest anxiety at work could be alleviated with one question.

- **Bring in outside speakers to work.** There are speakers on just about any subject. Contact your favorite author to come in and do a reading or a lecture. It will make work so much more interesting. I speak at companies and the employees always tell me how much they enjoy learning about health, wealth, and happiness.

- **Understand that happiness is a choice.** Just as in being healthy, you don't eat the right healthy foods by accident. You have to plan good eating choices. You don't exercise by accident. Nobody just happens to stumble onto a StairMaster on their way into a Krispy Kreme store. Happiness starts with you. Choose happiness at work and it will spread. Tell people at work that happiness should be a priority. Talk to management about a happiness plan. Give them this book. Open to this chapter. It will be fun to implement.
- **Memorize a great clean joke and use it.** Try out the joke with a friend or a spouse before you use it at work. Put the joke in your smartphone so you won't forget it. It is a great icebreaker. I even laugh at bad jokes. Keep it clean and inoffensive!
- **Prioritize your tasks.** Accomplish the most important things first. Even if they are the most unpleasant. There is only so much time each day. Putting off important tasks has been shown to increase anxiety. Being anxious means not being happy.
- **When you leave work, leave all your work problems behind.** You are more than just a paycheck and a job title. Refresh, rejuvenate, and relax. Work out or chill out. This is one of the most important things you can do to be happy at work. You must be happy outside of work.
- **Mentor a fellow coworker.** Being the new guy is tough. Karma is real. By being kind and sharing your friendship and experience with someone, one day someone will do the

same for you. The more you do this, the more friends you will have at work. The more friends you have at work, the happier you will be.

- **Avoid gossip.** Gossip tears people down. There are people in every office that hate being there. Avoid those people as much as you can. You want to foster a supportive atmosphere at your job. Spreading gossip will sabotage relationships and hurt people.
- **Have great off-sites.** Even if it is lunch in a nearby park, getting people out of the office can be fun. Fun manifests happiness.
- **Be the change you want to be at your job.** If there is low morale, you bring it up. If it is not fun, try to make it fun by having contests. Do whatever you can to change the environment. Encourage people.
- **Organize a charity day at work.** Have an off-site at a shelter. Build bicycles as a team-building exercise. My wife does things like these at Salesforce. Marc Benioff, the founder of Salesforce, invented the 1/1/1 Integrated Philanthropic model. Salesforce contributes 1 percent of employee hours, 1 percent of profits, and 1 percent of equity to the community. Marc Benioff is an incredible visionary and philanthropist.

Are you the hardest working person at your job? Why not? Are there designations or continuing education credits that you could earn? Find out your boss's weakness or what they don't want to do and become an expert at it. You need to create value as an employee and become indispensable. It's great to be wanted. Have you ever started a job and saw, right off the bat, the employees that were integral to the operation? You need to be one of those people. This will increase your respect amongst your peers. More important, it will increase your self-respect. Working hard will increase your happiness at work.

Do you fear that you are not qualified to look for a different job because you don't have a great resume or the right background? Are you afraid that you don't come from the right family to apply for your dream job? I'd like to tell you about Richard Lane.

As a baby, Richard Lane was found abandoned in a dumpster. Ella Lane, his foster mother, raised him. He played only one year of football at Scottsbluff Junior College in Nebraska. He went into the army and stayed there for four years. After he was discharged from the army, he went to work for an aircraft manufacturer. He hated it. He brazenly walked into the Los Angeles Rams' front office in 1952 and boldly asked for a tryout as a wide receiver. Blown away by his gall to presume he could play with players that had long resumes from the best schools and experienced NFL veterans, the Rams actually gave this no-name an opportunity as a cornerback one day at practice. This was not his natural position. He took his chance and made the most of it. He lined up at cornerback and their bruising running back ran right at him. Richard Lane knocked him out.

In his first year as a Rams cornerback, Richard Lane intercepted fourteen passes in twelve games. In 1952, the season was only twelve games long. He had never played cornerback before. This NFL interception record still stands today. He became known as "Night Train" Lane. You see, Richard Lane was petrified of flying. Football teams do a lot of traveling. He made sure that his play was so good that the team would let him travel by train separately. That's why they called him "Night Train."

This one-time nobody, junior-college dropout married Grammy award–winning jazz singer Dinah Washington. Hall of Fame basketball player Wilt Chamberlain was the best man at their wedding. She was inducted into the Rock and Roll Hall of Fame in 1993.

When Richard Lane retired, he worked for comedic genius Redd Foxx. Wanting to give back, he also worked for the Detroit Police Athletic League, mentoring underprivileged kids. *The Sporting News* named him the greatest defensive back of all time. In 2010, the NFL channel named him the number two greatest undrafted player of all time. He was enshrined in the Pro Football Hall of Fame in 1974.

What talents do you have that you are not currently using? Could you be like Night Train Lane and march into the employer of your dreams and demand a shot? How about starting your own company? What do you have to lose? The better question is what do you have to gain? Everything.

Make sure that whatever you do for work, do it with passion. In the movie *Jiro Dreams of Sushi*, Jiro Ono talks about making your career your calling. He was the first sushi-only restaurant to receive a Michelin three-star rating. His minimalist, ten-seat, humble restaurant is located in a Tokyo subway station. It takes months to get a reservation. People from around the world pay homage to this sushi master. His restaurant is extremely expensive, even for lunch. At eighty-five years old, he still dreams of perfecting the art of sushi. You have to be devoted to your career. If you don't like your job, find one that can be your calling. In the meantime, give your job your all. Treat it like it is your calling. Always take pride in your work and you will be happier.

CHAPTER 6

ASK YOURSELF GREAT QUESTIONS

Judge a man by his questions rather than by his answers.
—Voltaire

L et's say you are shopping for clothes and you come across a shirt that you like, but the price is outrageous. You can ask yourself, "Does this shirt look good on me?" The answer will probably be yes. Your credit card will take another hit and you will start a Down Cycle. The better, more rational question is, "Will this $150 shirt move me closer to financial independence or farther away?" People that are in debt and people that are overweight ask themselves the wrong questions.

By asking better questions, you can avoid a lot of trouble and pain. If you find yourself tempted to cheat on your spouse, a bad question to ask yourself is: "I wonder if that person is a good kisser?" Better questions to ask are: "What would happen to my life if this potential affair came to light? What would my wonderful spouse think of me? What terrible effect would this have on my beloved children? How would I be financially impacted?" When the horror of what could happen comes into your mind, your original silly question that most people who cheat ask themselves will seem completely irrelevant and foolish. I hope I have saved at least one marriage as a result of this paragraph.

Ask yourself the right questions throughout the day. This will help you analyze your current situation and maximize your life experience. Productivity and progress lead to happiness. When you are on a diet or trying to stay healthy, you should exercise. If you are sitting on the couch and watching TV, don't ask yourself, "What time does McDonald's close?" Instead, ask yourself, "What time does the gym close?" Another good question could be "Am I going to reach my goal of losing x pounds by watching another rerun of *Ace of Cakes*?"

If you are trying to lose weight, you shouldn't be watching shows like *Ace of Cakes*. It consciously and subconsciously programs your brain to want cake. Your brain is like a computer. If you watch shows about unhealthy food, you will eat unhealthy food. Every time you sit in front of the TV, ask yourself, "What can I watch that will make me happy, healthy, and more productive?" Shows about murder and crime are depressing. Shows about junk food lead to eating junk food. Watch shows that teach you something, like *Extreme Makeover: Weight Loss Edition* or *Bloomberg Risk Takers*.

One of my favorite shows is *Million Dollar Contractor*. My old classmate, Stephen Fanuka, is the star. I love it on so many levels. The first, of course, is seeing Steve achieve his dream. Steve is an incredible guy. We went to Archbishop Molloy High School together. He has an indomitable spirit. He always had a smile on his face and was always happy. How does a contractor get a nationwide television show? He believed in his dream and worked darn hard to get there.

The second reason to watch is because the show provides a blueprint for how dreams can be realized from someone's imagination. Most of the people he works for have worked very hard to get such a valuable home. He then transforms their idea into a reality. Along the way there are always problems that Steve has to overcome. There are cost overruns, labor problems, material problems, and deadlines. Like most things in life, things come together with enough elbow grease and belief in oneself.

The third level of satisfaction for me is the transformed space itself. I love interior design and beautiful homes. My father was a carpenter and we used to work together on ultra high-end apartments in Manhattan. I was his laborer. He worked me very hard. I saw how hard it was to make a living. I am grateful for that insight.

I also love how the show provides dreams for the viewers. Almost all of the show's viewers can't currently afford these homes. However, it gives them something to shoot for. He creates inspiring, habitable works of art. You can watch it with your children and say, "If you study really hard and apply yourself in life, that can be yours too!" People need inspiration so they can shake off their mediocrity and expect more from themselves.

The other great show is *Extreme Makeover: Weight Loss Edition*. These people lose, on average, over 200 pounds in one year. One of the participants lost 285 pounds in one year. He then regained twenty pounds in no time because he reverted to his old ways. To get back on track, he stopped driving to work because the temptation to pull over at a fast food place was too much. He took public transportation instead because he couldn't ask the driver to pull over and stop at a Mickey D's. He probably asked himself, "What do I need to do to keep me from pulling over at McDonald's?" The answer was use a form of transportation that eliminates temptation. That's the kind of dedication and problem solving that is necessary to maintain a weight loss. None of us are perfect. If it takes changing the way you get to work to keep the pounds off, do it. You must do whatever it takes.

Watching people stick to their diet and losing so much weight is incredibly inspirational. The participants are normal people like you and me that lost their way and are hundreds of pounds overweight. If they can lose from one hundred to 285 pounds in one year, you can lose twenty, thirty, forty, fifty, or more pounds in a year.

Anything is possible, especially when it comes to weight loss. This show is a family show. You can watch it with your kids. They can see how unhappy the participants are being overweight. They put everything on the table. They will talk about the most painful and personal things that tripped them up to get to their current weight. Then they will expound on how happy they are to be at a more normal weight.

You see, it's all about the questions we ask ourselves. We are judge and jury in our own minds. You need to ask the right questions in order to get the right outcomes. Instead of asking yourself "Can I?" ask yourself "How can I?" Don't be easy on yourself. Always strive to be better. Always be growing. Always be learning. Always be focused on improving. It's all about self-mastery.

CHAPTER 7

HOW TO BE HAPPY IN YOUR MARRIAGE AND OTHER LOVE RELATIONSHIPS

We are most alive when we are in love.
—JOHN UPDIKE

I have a great barber. His name is Mike and he is eighty-three years old. He is always happy and smiling. He is funny, lighthearted, and wise. I asked him while I was writing this book, what the secret was to his happiness. He said, "Easy, get a great spouse. That's half the battle right there!" He has been married to his wonderful wife for over fifty years.

Love is a crucial element of happiness. Every human being needs to be loved. If you are married, don't take your love for granted. Schedule a date night every week. You need time to build and renew your marriage.

Never say disparaging words to your loved one. They will always be remembered. You may say things in the heat of the moment, but they will live on forever. Being mean to your significant other is actually being mean to yourself.

You must forgive your partner. Nobody is perfect, including you. As Buddha once said, "Holding on to anger is like grasping a hot coal with the intent of throwing it at someone else; you are the one who gets burned." Move on from the hurt. Ask yourself, "Five years from now, will I really care that they forgot to take out the garbage for two weeks in a row?" If you forgive them, they will probably forgive you. You are giving yourself a get-out-of-jail-free card.

Do not argue. Communicate more effectively and compassionately. Try to see the other person's perspective. Take the high road and remember that when you are mean to people, you are actually hurting yourself. They will not want to be with you and you will feel guilty for a long time. Therefore nobody wins.

When talking to my wife, I use the acronym KLAP—kindness, love, and patience should always be at the front of your mind when talking to your spouse. Words can be like a tonic or a poison. I want my wife to be happy to see me when I come home at the end of the day. I want her to carry a favorable opinion of me throughout the day.

Think of your relationship with your loved one as a separate and distinct living entity, much like a flower. When you are verbally abusive or constantly complaining about your spouse, you are sapping the life energy from that beautiful flower. Your relationship needs to be nourished in order to flourish. Don't kill it with negative energy and unkind words.

Think back to the time when you longed for a loving relationship. You would have done anything to have love in your life. Relationships are a blessing. There are so many lonely people out there that are suffering from a lack of partnership. If you have someone in your life that cares about you, it is imperative that you discipline yourself, no matter how at your wits' end or tired you are, to communicate with kindness, love, and patience.

I didn't meet my wonderful wife until I was thirty-four. When Shannon came along, I knew ten minutes into our first date that she was my soul mate. She was so beautiful, intelligent, kind, and funny. We clicked. Even though she is my soul mate and I love her with all my heart, I still get frustrated at times. That's natural. Thankfully, she doesn't always see life from my angle or perspective. In prior relationships, I would fight to be right and have my way. Those relationships never worked out. Those relationships are dead. Funny how that works.

Because I was older and more mature when I met my wife, I decided that I would never let this valuable relationship die. I would always approach conflict with kindness, love, and patience. I would let this proud Irish-American male lose some disagreements with dignity. I would let my gorgeous wife win. Guess what? I am the happiest I have ever been in a relationship!

Inspirational speaker Tavis Smiley said, "I told my wife that if she ever leaves me…I'm coming with her!" That's how invested in a love relationship you have to be. I often tell this joke to people when they meet me for the first time. It sums me up as a person who keeps his word. That's how much I love my wife. I am "all in" on my marriage. I have surrendered myself to my wife. We have become one unit, one force for good in this universe.

Never say the "D word." My wife and I made a deal at the beginning of our relationship. We promised that we would never say the word "divorce" in connection with our relationship. I will be married to my wife for as long as we both shall live. We may have our differences along the way about a lot of things, but we have promised that we will work them out, no matter how long it takes. As far as I'm concerned, I am truly blessed to have my wife. I am not going to waste that blessing on pride, foolishness, or any other silly notion. We are going to get through whatever difficulty arises with the other by our side. I look forward to being next to my wife as our grandchildren play at our feet. I look forward to family vacations to far-off exotic destinations. I look forward to the feeling of satisfaction that we didn't lose sight of the precious gift of love that we were given many years before. With the mindset that nothing can defeat us and there is no other alternative than to stay together, I know that all of my marital dreams can come true, because they are already coming true.

Renovate your marriage and love relationships. I used to see firsthand how houses could undergo a dramatic transformation from old and dated to fresh and vibrant when I would go out and work with my dad, the master carpenter.

A great renovation TV show is *Property Brothers*. The show focuses on the Scott twins. Drew Scott is a realtor and Jonathan Scott is a licensed contractor. Their clients can't afford new or updated houses. They show their clients old houses that have been neglected and run down. They convince their clients that what they see now can be radically restored and made beautiful. Almost all of the clients are skeptical. They just do not believe that something so old and worn out could become beautiful again. After tons of hard work and patience, the clients walk into their new, beautiful homes. Most of them start to cry. They are overjoyed. They can't believe that what they saw before could ever have become what they have now.

You can do this with your relationships. What may seem like an impossible task can be completely turned around and made whole. Miracles can be accomplished with difficult work and dedication. With kindness, love, and patience, what once was thought dead can be resurrected. A relationship that once was thought intractable and unsalvageable can be reborn into a beautiful and incredibly precious gift.

Sometimes you value things more that were almost lost. When you see something slipping away and you make a valiant effort to turn the tide at great personal expense, you will not let it go again. Do this with the one you love. Start with baby steps. I have a friend who treats his wife every morning with coffee in bed. Every morning she wakes up to her husband's love. His wife loves him so much for this and many other small kindnesses that he sows in their relationship. Try doing this with your loved one. Breakfast in bed shouldn't be just a once-a-year thing.

Don't confuse small with insignificant. Small can be greatly important. In relationships, the small leads to the big, in the positive and the negative. That's why you should always be honest with your partner. A small fib that is found out can lead to great mistrust. Mistrust can lead to disaster.

Dates nights are not just for single people. We have a babysitter every Saturday night. My kids love having a babysitter. I love Saturday night. It's my favorite night of the week. We usually spend it watching a movie and having dinner in San Francisco. The restaurants in San Francisco are to die for. You can get every kind of food in every kind of neighborhood. There is always a new restaurant to try. You can get great, healthy, organic food everywhere. It's usually local food too. If you've never been to San Francisco, do yourself a favor and go.

Date nights are like mini-vacations for your marriage. It is your time to rekindle and remember why you got together before the kids. My wife can forget all the pressures of the day, let down her hair, and laugh. She can be young again. The only big decision she has to make is which restaurant she wants to go to. It is great to see her so happy and carefree. When she is happy, I'm happy. It's true what they say: Happy wife, happy life. It's an investment in one of your most important priorities: your marriage.

Instead of focusing on your spouse's bad qualities, focus on their good qualities. Everyone has something great about them. Make a list of all the great things about your spouse. When they annoy you, tell them they are a wonderful person. They possess great skill at such and such. Then let them know that this current behavior hurts you and they need to change whatever they are doing. Tell them you are stating this from a place of love. By starting with a compliment and saying a kind thing, your partner will be less inclined to get hurt and then turn around and hurt you. Honest communication is important, but a spoonful of sugar really does help the medicine go down. Do not yell at your spouse.

You need to compliment your partner daily. Say "I love you" every day, twice a day. Make sure that your significant other knows that they are appreciated and loved, and it will come back to you. They will see how happy you make them and they will return the favor. This will create a cycle of love that will make you happy.

Break old patterns. Do unexpected, kind things for each other. If it is their turn to do the dishes, tell them to go relax and you do the dishes. I know some wives out there may get so confused that they faint or call the police and claim that someone has body-snatched their husband. Make your partner a nice hot cup of tea to relax them before bed. Send them a text during the day saying that they are great-looking, sexy, successful, and wonderful. Compliment them publicly on Facebook. Love them passionately and unrelentingly. Always let them know how much they mean to you.

I tell my wife every day that she is beautiful. The truth is that she is beautiful. She deserves to hear the truth. I spent my whole childhood listening to my father compliment my mother. He treated my mother like she was Sophia Lauren. He is a master at complimenting people. Guess what? Everybody loves my dad! He taught me to be respectful and kind. He explained to me that macho men are insecure, low intelligence, fools. A real man loves his wife and treats her with respect, all the days of her life.

Men need compliments too. Just because you are involved with a big burly man does not mean he has a heart made of stone. Men need to know that they are loved and cherished as well. It makes our chest swell out. We can walk out the door and take on the world knowing that we have someone that cares about us. We have someone worth fighting tooth and nail for. It is a tough world out there. We need to know that we are in a relationship that is worth all the effort. All these wonderful things can be accomplished with just a few magical, kind words.

CHAPTER 8

HOW TO BE HAPPY WITH YOUR KIDS

*There really are places in the heart you don't
even know exist until you love a child.*
—ANNE LAMOTT

I have been blessed with two amazing and wonderful kids. They are incredibly bright and inquisitive children. They get bored easily, which is a big challenge. You have to always keep them interested. Making average things into games and adventures is a way to do this. On Saturdays, we do something we call "Duffy family adventure day." My wife charges me with "making the magic" and I look on the Internet to see what is going on that day in the Bay Area. I have sites like RedTri, Bay Area Parent, and SFgate bookmarked on my computer. There is usually something interesting to do. Even if it is just a farmers market, I still exude enthusiasm, as if it is the most intriguing activity in the world to do. Children feed off your enthusiasm. If you act excited, they will be excited.

How do you get a four-year-old to watch the Olympics for two hours? You throw an Olympics party! It's not a real party, in the traditional sense; it's just the family. My wife and I are big fans of the Olympics. I love to see people commit themselves to a goal and try to attain it no matter what. I want my children to emulate that kind of self-sacrifice.

During the London Olympics, the four of us would get in bed and pick a country or an athlete to root for. We could all pick the same athlete if we wanted. If your athlete won, you got a small treat or a hug. My kids loved it. They paid attention to the announcer's tips on who the favorites were. They watched the back-story segments to gain an edge. The athlete's stories usually dealt with how the person overcame adversity to rise to such a high level. It showed my children that greatness and self-mastery are possible if effort is expended. I explained to them that these truths carry over to real life outside of the games. Watching the Olympics also showed them that even countries that are at war can coexist in peace to achieve a higher goal. This is one of the greatest things you can watch with your children.

Most children don't like going to bed. Mine are no exception. I decided to come up with a way that would have them looking forward to it. My kids love to dance, so every night we have a dance party. I play child-appropriate music for around three to four minutes. It's just one song. If they complain or act up, they lose the dance party. It's a way to keep them behaving well and to create memories. I look forward every night to our dance party. We have made up our own dance moves like "backwards dance" where I hold their hands and have them walk backwards while holding them up off the floor. We also do the "Spider Man" dance where I carefully throw them onto a bed filled with pillows and they fly through the air like Spider Man. We all laugh so hard and enjoy each other's company immensely.

Laugh and the whole world laughs with you. Cry and you cry alone. My mother and father drummed that into my head. They had no time for my nonsense when I was a child. It was great training and great love. They would shun me if I cried because I wanted something that was bad for me. They would embrace me if I made them laugh. Guess what I did?

As a parent, it takes great love to punish a child. I love my children so much it hurts and I want them to know it at all times. However, you run the risk of spoiling your children if you make them your friend and give in to their every want and desire. You will unleash a selfish, argumentative, misfit into the world. You are not doing them a favor by spoiling them. It all starts with you. Take your responsibility seriously. You will be tremendously rewarded in your old age if you raise unselfish children.

Raise your children as givers. I am blessed with wonderful in-laws. When my beloved mother-in-law, Pam, was going through chemotherapy after having a mastectomy, I had my kids do a "secret mission" with me. I told them that we were going to get Grandma a love package so she knows we love her and to make her feel better. I purposely put off buying the candy and flowers for two days to have the excitement of doing good build in them for two days. I would say, "Grandma, Mikey and Kendall will be going on a secret mission soon. We can't tell you what it is about because it's a secret!" The kids would pipe up with enthusiasm and say, "Yeah, Grandma, you're really going to like it!"

It was so cute to see them in a position of giving and enjoying the role. When we did get the flowers and the See's candy (which is her favorite), the kids were so excited to give it to their grandma. They were so happy that they could make her feel better. It was so touching to see a grandmother's love as she hugged them and cried tears of joy. Teach your children that givers gain.

I have read many books on child psychology. I strongly considered becoming a child psychologist while I was studying psychology. Over the years, I have read many articles and studies that contradict one another regarding how to raise happy children. This I know for sure: love your children and laugh with your children. Then laugh with your children and then love your children some more. Repeat. Repeat. Repeat. I don't know who gets more out of it, the parent or the child.

J. M. Barrie, the author of *Peter Pan*, wrote, "When the first baby laughed for the first time, its laugh broke into a thousand pieces, and they all went skipping about, and that was the beginning of fairies." There is no consistent higher level of joy than holding your child in your arms as you both break your heart laughing. That's how I was raised. It works. There is no antidepressant more powerful than your child's "joy laugh." The joy laugh comes when all of their defenses are down and they surrender to the humor that has overtaken their body. They are powerless to resist. They throw their head back and let it all go. There are no pretenses, no angling for a want, just pure joy and unbridled happiness. I live for those moments. Those laughs are the closest thing to heaven on earth. All is right in the universe. I have done my job as a parent.

Try to make friends with the parents of your children's friends. When you get together, your kids will be happy and so will you. They will be off playing together while you get to enjoy having adult conversations. Everybody wins! My wonderful sister Roisin taught me that. She and the parents of her children's friends go on vacation together and have incredible fun adventures. They have pool parties and barbecues. When you spend time with other parents, you can get great tips on local camps, the best schools, the best doctors to use, and which to avoid. You get all of this while having fun and providing a safe environment for your kids to grow up in. Everybody wins!

One warm August night, before putting my kids to bed, my daughter asked me what day it was. It touched my heart. I walked over to the couch and sat beside her. I asked her what time it was. She said that she didn't know how to tell time. In two days, she would start the third grade. She would learn shortly. I said, "Kendall, one day soon, you will know all too well what day it is and what time it is and how much you own. Do you have any worries about money?" She said, "No." I said, "I will remind you of this conversation and you will probably deny it or won't even believe that there was a time when money wasn't a concern. But for now I will enjoy this moment in time when the only thing you care about is going to bed too early. I will remember you as a beautiful burst of sunshine with unlimited energy. Every night, running away from the dinner table early to put on shows with Mikey in the kitchen for your gorgeous young mommy and me, laughing and dancing and not caring about what you looked like or being cool. I will remember when I took you to church and you asked me if you could put all six dollars of your allowance in the box instead of just one to light a candle for your baby cousin in the hospital. On the ride home, you asked me why you felt so incredibly happy. It was at that moment that you realized the joy of giving." She looked at me with her tiny, stunning, glorious, and resplendent little face and said, "Daddy, I love you." She gave me a great big hug with all of her eight-year-old strength. Like every other parent, I wished dearly that that moment could last forever. It always will.

CHAPTER 9

FAITH AND HAPPINESS

To believe in things you can see and touch is no belief at all. To believe in the unseen is a triumph and a blessing.
—Abraham Lincoln

Whether you believe in a Higher Power, God, the universe, or something else, having faith in something greater than you can give you a purpose in life. Understanding the point of our existence can lead to happiness. Studies have consistently shown that people that believe in God score higher on happiness tests.

As I've said, my father is the happiest person I know. He wakes up at five in the morning and prays. He gets out of bed and opens his local church. At eighty-two years young, he is the altar boy, the lector, and the Eucharistic minister. He also goes out and gives communion to the sick, the dying, and the homebound. He is not afraid of dying and never has been. He is convinced that one day he will be reunited with my mother in heaven. He doesn't have worries. Whenever he has a problem, he gives it to God. He always has and always will be happy. He says that his faith is the cornerstone of his happiness.

Everybody loves my dad. He loves everybody. Whenever I call him, we break our hearts laughing. I can only call him at home or in my car. I can't call him at work, because I always end up howling.

My sides hurt when I get off the phone. My father never complains, though his poor hands are twisted with rheumatoid arthritis and he can hardly hold a glass. He has never told me about his arthritis pain. I've asked him about it and he waives me off with a hand that looks like a three-year-old sculptor made it, saying that it is nothing. He will then make a joke and change the subject. That's when my sides start hurting again. That's my dad. He's the happiest man alive, with a faith as strong as iron.

Faith gives people hope. With hope, one is able to take risks. By taking risks, one can advance in love, career, and life. St. Paul wrote in Philippians 4:13, "I can do all things through Him who strengthens me." Believe that you can do all things through God. Studies have shown that people who have faith live longer, get sick less, and recover faster than those that do not.

One of the hardest parts of living is dealing with death. When a loved one passes away, it is very comforting to know that it is not the end for them. To have a belief that one day you will be reunited with them in a better place is what gets most people through this ordeal. Faith in an afterlife can help people stay motivated to be good and kind in this life.

Joining a faith-based community, regardless of type, is a soul-nourishing endeavor. It can be a little nerve wracking at first, especially if you don't know anyone there. The reward is manifold, however. You get friends that are of like mind and values. You get to surround yourself with people of morals and principles. You get to raise your children in a great environment. You get to deepen your faith and learn from older and younger people the right path to follow. You stretch yourself in the right way.

Going to worship is working out for your soul. You just feel better after it. You hear words of wisdom you don't hear on TV. You get to learn ways of dealing with the world that benefit you and society.

Your house of worship probably has its own or supports some type of charity. When you give back to your community, your soul soars. You feel alive and joyful. You are the one that receives your charity. Do-gooders know this. That's why they never stop helping people, because they are helping themselves. They are helping their own soul.

If you have been thinking about joining a local faith-based group, do it! I guarantee you won't be sorry. It will plug you into your community. You will see people from your faith community all over town. I can't walk down the street without getting a big wave from someone from my church. That makes me so happy. I feel like I'm in Mayberry. As a former New Yorker that used to watch *The Andy Griffith Show,* I just laugh every time I bump into someone at Starbucks or get honked at by a church member. It feels great to be known and appreciated. That is what a happy life is all about— good friends that you cherish and respect.

My church has a men's club. I used to think that church men's clubs were for really, really old men that were really, really boring. That couldn't be further from the truth. I signed up for the men's club's golf trip several years ago. I didn't know anybody. I got on the bus and everybody passed me by. Boy, did I feel uncomfortable. Then the town dentist sat next to me. He took a genuine interest in me. Soon enough, other men came by and introduced themselves. I still felt a little nervous, but I forced myself to endure and take a chance.

Today, I know these great gentlemen well. They are fabulous people that have enriched my life so much. We meet every month at the church hall. We have dinner and a great speaker. Among the many incredible speakers who have come to talk to us are the assistant GM of the San Francisco Giants, Conrad Ray; the coach of the Stanford Men's golf team, Dick Davey; a men's basketball coach at Stanford, Russell Turner; the head coach of UC Irvine men's bas-ketball, Daniel Descalso, who won a world series ring with the St. Louis Cardinals in 2011; Jeff Clark, who started the Mavericks big wave surf competition; and a secret service agent. We raise money for charity. It is great. Take a chance. Attend a meeting where you don't know anyone and see what happens when you allow yourself to open up. You have only one life. Spend it with good people, productively. Happiness will follow you like a hungry little lapdog.

CHAPTER 10

GIVING AND HAPPINESS

For it is in giving that we receive.
—FRANCIS OF ASSISI

Give. The sooner you understand that word, the happier you will be. Always be generous with your time and money. Irish-American Chuck Feeney has been called "the James Bond of philanthropy" because he was so secretive for so long about his charitable donations. He is one of the greatest givers in the history of the world. According to Forbes, he has given away over $6,200,000,000! He plans to give away another $1,300,000,000 by 2016. He plans to die broke. This is just the opposite of what most people do with their money. Instead of stockpiling money, he lives very frugally. He flies coach. He wears a black plastic Casio watch.

In one of the few interviews he has granted, Chuck Feeney told *Forbes* magazine, "People used to ask me how I got my jollies, and I guess I'm happy when what I'm doing is helping people and unhappy when what I'm doing isn't helping people." He said, "People who have money have an obligation." According to Bill Gates, Feeney is the inspiration for Bill Gates' foundation and the Giving While Living Pledge. Bill Gates said, "Chuck Feeney is a remarkable role model and the ultimate example of giving while living." Not bad for a kid from a blue-collar neighborhood in New Jersey.

Chuck Feeney was born in Elizabeth, New Jersey, on April 23, 1931. He was in the armed services during the Korean War. When he got out, he started selling liquor to navy personnel overseas. He used the G.I. Bill to go to college at Cornell. It is estimated that he has given over $900,000,000 to Cornell. He has also given around $1,000,000,000 to Irish education.

He is one of the founders of Duty Free Shoppers (DFS) Group. These are the shops you see in airports all over the world. In 1982, he started his foundation, Atlantic Philanthropies. In 1984 he transferred his stake in DFS to the Atlantic Philanthropies. DFS was later sold to LVMH for over $1,600,000,000.

Chuck doesn't believe in dying with your wealth. He said, "I cannot think of a more personally rewarding and appropriate use of wealth than to give while one is living—to personally devote oneself to meaningful efforts to improve the human condition. More importantly, today's needs are so great and varied that intelligent philanthropic support and positive interventions can have greater value and impact today than if they are delayed when the needs are greater." Be like Chuck. You can't take it with you. At least get the satisfaction of seeing your hard work accomplish something while you are alive.

Some Native American cultures have a practice called "keeping the gift in motion." If somebody did something nice for you, you were supposed to turn around and do something nice for someone else. Then that person would continue the chain of good events. The important thing was to not be the person who let the motion of the gift stop with them. You were shunned if you allowed the gift to stop. It was an exciting thing to watch the gift morph between generations. If you ever wondered what the native peoples did before TV, this was one thing.

Try this with your kids. Explain to them about keeping the gift in motion. I did this with my four-year-old son, Mike. He liked listening to the stories of Indians living in teepees and riding horses. I then introduced the concept of keeping the gift in motion. He jumped up and ran out of the room. He yelled, "Mommy, I want to help you!" He came back in the room and asked me in all earnestness, "Will this keep the gift in the ocean?" He was so excited to help. You must take time and put down your laptop to teach your children these crucial life lessons. Facebook can wait.

An ancient Hindu proverb states, "True happiness consists in making others happy." Volunteering makes people happy. I was in the Contact Program while I was a freshman at Georgia Tech to become a Marist brother. Growing up, my father was the lector at Ascension church in Elmhurst, New York. My sisters were in the choir and I was an altar boy. During high school at Archbishop Molloy, I volunteered my summers at the Marist brother's facility in Esopus in upstate New York. I worked with special needs adults and kids. Some of the campers were paralyzed and were in wheelchairs. They needed every facet of their existence cared for. They needed to be spoon-fed, showered, clothed, and so on. This was their parents' only two-week break from their children. The feeling of happiness and joy I had at the end of the camp was incredible. It was the closest thing to heaven I have ever experienced.

CHAPTER 11

REGRETS

*As you grow older, you'll find the only things
you regret are the things you didn't do.*
—ZACHARY SCOTT

Regrets. I've had a few. But then again, too few to mention.
—FRANK SINATRA

I had to have the double quote there to honor my dad. We saw Sinatra at Carnegie Hall when I was fourteen. He was fantastic. Talk about a man that lived a full life! Although Sinatra was by far an imperfect person, he did seize life by the horns. He wasn't afraid to travel the world and take chances, whether it was acting, singing, dancing, or telling jokes in front of gigantic audiences. There was even a time in his career when his popularity waned. He lost his looks and his hair. He kept going. He never gave up. He stayed true to himself and kept working and refining his skills.

We should all be like Frank when it comes to his bravery and courage. He had swagger. He left it all out there. No regrets. I once asked Paul Anka what Sinatra was like. Paul was friends with him and cowrote Sinatra's most famous song, "My Way." Paul said he was a great, one of a kind man.

We cannot change the past. There is no point in living there. There is no point in living with regret. Regret is an anchor that keeps us from moving forward and enjoying the present. Regret is an invisible captor that taunts us as we grip invisible bars. Regret is a jail that has no walls, only willing captives. Suffering is the only reward of regret. Forgiveness is the only cure.

What do you regret the most? According to a study by the British Heart Foundation, lack of exercise and travel are the two biggest regrets. The study found that the average respondent had six regrets. They also had the equivalent of about five days a year dwelling on them. Five days a year wasted on regretting something! Instead of regretting, start doing. One in three people in the study regretted not traveling.

In today's world of discount airfare, travel reward points, and last-minute deals on the Internet, there is no reason not to travel. The secret to economy travel is planning. Stay with a friend or a family member. Organize a trip with a group and your airfare and hotel could be free. Book a hotel with a free breakfast and do brunch. Then just eat dinner at a local place using apps like Yelp to give you recommendations of restaurants that have great food and low prices. Bring a water bottle with you as you tour.

The following table lists some common regrets and what you can do to remedy the situation.

REGRETS	REMEDY
Lack of travel	Plan and go on a vacation.
Lack of exercise	Get a workout partner and hold each other accountable to your goals.

REGRETS	REMEDY
Not keeping in touch with friends	Plan monthly get-togethers, which include physical activity like volleyball or a friend jog-a-thon with dollar store prizes.
Missed out on marrying the love of your life	Get over it and find someone who will be delighted to marry you.
Did not reach an educational goal	Go back to school now. Do it online if you are busy.
Did not get a promotion	Apply yourself to your job now. Start a new and better career as your own boss.
Never made enough money	Do something you love for a living in your spare time. Then make that career your job.
Never told someone you loved them	Pick up the phone and tell them. If they are not alive, pray for them.

Below, please write your regrets and then write what you are going to do about it to release you from this unnecessary jail.

REGRETS   **REMEDY**

_____

_____

_____

_____

_____

_____

Any goal can be achieved. You just have to use your mind and ask yourself good questions. Use the Internet to get tips on whatever it is you need to do. Ask mentors who have already accomplished your goal for their opinion. People love to give advice because most people are helpful and good. Do not feel bad about asking people for help. People want to help you. It makes them feel good. It's a total win-win.

As far as lost loves are concerned, there is a reason why you never married or stayed with that person. Let it go at that. Do not carry around the burden of "What if?" All things happen for a reason. If today you are not with a person you once loved and lost through infidelity, long distance, or death, there is a reason. Our obligation is to maximize every waking moment, *today*. Living in the present circumstances is where you can maximize your future. The past is gone. Love the person that is your current partner with extreme intensity or make it your purpose to go find someone to love. What a waste of time and energy regret can be!

The time to make your dreams come true is now. Psychologist Dr. Gayle Brewer, PhD said, "Many of us seem resigned to the idea that it is impossible to live out our dreams for a variety of reasons. Often it's not seizing opportunities that we regret. And it's not until later that we realize how important they really were. We can be guilty of putting things off but don't realize that later in life we will not have the time to pursue them."

So don't let the time on your clock run out before you realize your purpose and your dreams. I work with a lot of older, successful people. They have a lot fewer regrets than people who are less successful because they took action. They put down the remote and wrote a business plan. They left the bar after two drinks or did not go there at all. They were able to put their kids through college and still have enough left over to retire on their terms. They lived life to the fullest because they did not give in to fear.

Sometimes if you change your perspective on regret, great things can come of it, including peace and a willingness to help others. One of the greatest stories I have ever heard of someone changing their perspective on an absolutely horrific ordeal into something of value is Katie Beers. It gives me shivers to even think about what this poor girl went through only to come out of it with what she describes as "the best thing that ever happened to me."

Katie Beers was kidnapped at the age of ten in 1993. She was chained for more than two weeks in a coffin-size box in a New York dungeon. Some twenty years later, she cowrote a book called *Buried Memories: Katie Beers' Story* with the reporter that had covered her story back when the kidnapping happened. Katie Beers says her story has a happy ending.

She was abused from the time she was a toddler by her extended family. When she was rescued from her captivity, she was put in a foster home with a loving family in East Hampton, Long Island. She later went to college and got a degree in business. She met her wonderful husband in college and had two great kids of her own. She has a good job in Pennsylvania in the insurance industry.

In an interview with the AP she said, the kidnapping was "The best thing that happened to me. I would have never gotten out of the abuse situation I was in. There's no point really in me right now being sad or wondering what if. I try not to be sad about what happened, because ultimately it made me who I am today, and I'm very satisfied and happy with my life."

When asked about her book she said, "I hope that more does come out of the book. I would love to be able to help other kids or adults or to be an inspirational or motivational speaker, something like that. But if I go back to my life in rural Pennsylvania and go back to my insurance sales job I would love that, too. I'm very happy with where I'm at."

Think about the worst things that have happened to you. Do they compare to a childhood of abuse and eventually being kidnapped and tortured in a dungeon? I'm guessing probably not. Change your perspective on these bad memories. Instead of regretting what happened to you, can you find it in your heart to understand that they have produced some good in your life today? Be like Katie Beers and see the positive in your negative circumstances.

When it comes to regret, you need to be like a pitcher in baseball. You have to have a short memory. I have never seen a pitcher in baseball not take the field because he was burned for a homerun in the prior inning. I have never heard an announcer say, "Well, that's it, ladies and gentlemen. The team has given up and thrown in the towel because they didn't play so well and things aren't going in their favor. Thank you for watching this extremely shortened broadcast today. The manager regrets that he put the wrong pitcher in and even with half a game to go, he can't forgive himself for the mistake. But you know how it goes, why not quit when you're down by one run!" Even the best athletes expect that they will not always be perfect in their play. Michael Jordan lost plenty of basketball games and kept on going, getting better and better.

I met motivational speaker, singer, and author Tom Sullivan after he spoke at a symposium at Oracle in Redwood City, California. He is brilliant, warm, and funny. His speech about his life made people laugh and cry, then cry and laugh. He ended his talk with a great song. He blew the room away. He walked off the stage to a thunderous standing ovation. He is an incredible man that has accomplished things that most people could not do in ten lifetimes. If you ever get a chance to see him speak, he will change your life forever, for the better.

Tom Sullivan was born blind. He is actually *grateful* to be blind. In an article by Sami Martin in the *Christian Post* in 2012, Tom

Sullivan said, "Philosophically, I decided that the best thing that ever happened to me is that I am blind. I would have been living in Boston, a lawyer, doctor or teacher and had a fine life, but I wouldn't have written 14 books, 90 TV show series, a movie about my life... wouldn't have spoken to 4,000–5,000 corporations. I was born in 1947—had I been born three years before that, I would have been dead: no incubators. Three years later, I would have been able to see."

When you let go of regrets and reposition your disadvantages to become your advantage, like Tom Sullivan did, you can actually go higher than you could have ever thought or imagined. To me, the third word of the previous quote is the most powerful. He *decided* that the best thing that ever happened to him is that he is blind. You have to make a decision to give up regret. You have to shift your perspective from one of regret to one that helps you achieve.

So please keep on going forward with strength and power. Understand that life is short and you always need to be looking ahead and not behind. Take down the rearview mirror of regret from your life. Yes, learn from your mistakes, but don't let the mistakes of your past keep you from participating in the game of life that is going on around you right now. Everyone has regrets. Instead of focusing on your failures, focus on what you have done right and build on that. Strive for excellence and not perfection. The most successful people act like Thomas Edison and see each failure as a step closer to their victory. If you are not failing, you are not trying. So keep on trying!

CHAPTER 12

MEDITATION AND HAPPINESS

Meditation is painful in the beginning, but it bestows immortal Bliss and supreme joy in the end.
—SWAMI SIVANANDA

Hundreds of scientific studies have confirmed that meditation can increase the pleasurable part of human existence and decrease the negative. It has psychological, spiritual, and physiological benefits. There are many different forms of meditation. There are also many different uses and traditions of meditation. Meditation has been around for thousands of years. Almost all faiths and hundreds of millions of people practice it.

The psychological benefits include: greater focus, increased productivity, increased clarity, and relief of stress and anxiety. I meditate every day for about three minutes. I clear my mind by focusing on my breathing. I then start to plan my day. I see what I want to accomplish. I see myself happy and productive. I see myself having a positive impact on other people. I see myself making other people laugh and smile. I see myself extending love, kindness, and gratitude. Guess what? That's what happens!

The subconscious mind is always working. If you program your subconscious mind to be positive through meditation, it will be positive. If you ignore your subconscious mind, it will fill itself up with paranoia and other stimuli that you are taking in through the Internet and the news (which is almost always negative). Meditating helps you choose which emotions and information to plug in to your subconscious mind.

Other psychological benefits include entering a state of calm. We are a society of multi-taskers. This is a new phenomenon to the human body. This is not our normal state. From the dawn of time until cell phones showed up, farmers farmed. They weren't listening to the radio on a giant GPS-guided tractor and talking on the phone with their commodities broker in a different time zone, while their wife texted them that their son failed math again. We are less than we can be by diverting our attention to so many things at once. Our nervous system starts to get overloaded and can literally break down. Nervous breakdowns are real. They are also really frightening. Take the time to mediate. It only takes a few minutes. It can reboot your nervous system and make you more productive.

Physiological benefits include strengthening the mind-body connection. We have been taught to ignore our bodies. We are told to, "Suck it up! Walk it off!" Meditating helps put you back in touch with your body. It can rejuvenate you and help your body be ready for the coming day. It can relax it for a better night's sleep.

Can't sleep? Meditate. If you replay all that went wrong during the day, you will exhaust your body by persecuting your mind with "what if's." What if I said something better to my boss? What if I had worked out instead of eating that entire extra cheese pizza? All the questions that you torture yourself with every night only harm you. You then replay all of these troubling issues in your dreams and nightmares. Relax, meditate, and forgive your perfectly imperfect self.

Meditation also helps you be more spiritual. It can provide peace of mind. It helps you understand yourself more. It gives you a more positive attitude about life. It definitely helps keep you in the present moment. It can make you feel like you took a nap. It can help accelerate enlightenment.

Here is a simple way to meditate:

1. Sit down. The easiest position to meditate in is sitting. You can close the door to your office, close your eyes on the bus, or bring a pillow to the top of a mountain. Meditating at work is a great way to relieve stress and energize you for the rest of the day. Just a few minutes will do wonders for you. Meditating in nature, especially by the water brings you in harmony with the world.

2. Relax. Close your eyes and let all your muscles relax. Let go of any tightness in your face, neck, and shoulders. Relax your muscles, starting at the top of your head and moving down. You would be amazed at the amount of energy we spend keeping our body so tense.

3. Breathe. Focus on your breathing. Breathe through your nose. Feel the cool air enter your nose and exit warmer. Breathe from your tummy. Breathe slowly and deeply.

4. Enter into a state of calm. By focusing on your breathing, you can start to push out other thoughts that are running through your mind. There will be times when you are stressed, when your mind will not let you completely focus. That's normal. Understand and accept this phenomenon. Just keep bringing your focus back to your breathing. Be patient. At the very least, you have relaxed the muscles in your body. You will feel better as a result. Calm thoughts like "I am relaxed, everything is good" will put you in a state of calm. Also, visualizing your favorite places like the beach or a Hawaiian waterfall can help you calm down.

5. End your meditation slowly. When it is time to come back to reality, do it slowly. Start to focus on the sounds of your surroundings. Focus on the most distant sound and then the closest sound. Slowly open your eyes and stretch your hands over your head. Stretch your neck by tilting your head from side to side.

There are different uses for meditation. Sports psychologists use meditation to help athletes become the best that they can be. They also use it to increase their focus and reduce anxiety. Can you imagine attempting a game-winning field goal from sixty yards out with the whole world watching? I was lucky enough to kick a field goal in the Dallas Cowboys billion-dollar stadium during a tour of the facility. The only people watching me kick were other tourists. I felt a lot of pressure not to look stupid. That pressure works against you in terms of performance. I should know. I blew the kick!

Here are some meditations you can try.

Meditation on a goal. Choose a goal that you would like to achieve or an ideal outcome that you are looking for. During the meditation, when you enter a state of calm in step 4, experience the emotions that would occur if the goal were achieved. In your imagination, imagine what you would see if it took place. Imagine it as if you were watching a video of it taking place. See yourself in the video. Where are you? Who are you with? Soak in the positive emotions if this ideal outcome had actually taken place. What would you feel, emotionally and physically? Focus on those joyful emotions. Ask yourself what could I do to make this happen? What would I need to do or say in order for this outcome to come to pass? Reflect on the answers that surfaced. Then slowly exit the meditation, using step 5.

I believe that happiness is a choice. You have to choose to be happy. One of the ways you can achieve happiness is to program your subconscious mind using a happiness meditation.

Meditation for happiness. As you enter a state of calm, imagine you are in a beautiful green meadow. You can smell the jasmine and the lavender as you breathe in through your nose. It is a beautiful, brilliant sunny day. It is not too hot or too cold. You are wearing the most comfortable clothes. Everything is perfect. There is nothing to be done. You are there with someone you love. You find yourself by a big oak tree with a swing that seats two people. You sit in the swing next to your loved one. You gently rock back and forth with your eyes closed while focusing on the gentle breeze that cools your face. You tilt your head back and listen to the laughter of your loved one enjoying the simple motion of the swing. You take your loved one by the hand. Waiting for you on the other side of the tree is a red-checkered picnic blanket. On the blanket are all of your favorite foods and drinks. You speak to your loved one and tell them how much you appreciate them. They return the favor and explain in detail what makes you so special to them. You reflect on those positive thoughts as you slowly start to regain your consciousness.

The following is a meditation that I learned at Stanford during a course taught by the incredible Dr. Laura Delizonna, PhD. She is a wonderful, outspoken advocate for happiness. It is a fun one to do.

Meditation for self-worth. Imagine it is your eightieth birthday. All of the important people in your life speak about how great you are and how you made such a positive impact in their life. It is kind of like a roast, but everything said is positive. You are the star of the evening. Everything is fabulous and everyone is happy. Everyone is there to honor you. You can feel the love in this opulent room, packed with the finest people, food, and drink. Your family is there:

friends, schoolmates, teachers, coworkers, and neighbors. They will list all of your achievements. What are they saying about you into the microphone? What positive things would they say about your personality, your contributions, your work, and your friendship? What did they admire about you? What difference did you make in their lives and the lives of others? Reflect on what they say as you slowly open your eyes.

There is no right way or wrong way to meditate. The important thing is that you do it several times a week. There will be days that you won't be able to enter a calm state. Make sure that you breathe deeply whether meditating or not. Breathing deeply helps your body obtain the correct amount of oxygen and keeps you more relaxed.

CHAPTER 13

THE HAPPINESS FORMULA:
PURPOSE + PROGRESS = HAPPINESS

*The meaning of life is to find your gift; the
purpose of life is to give it away.*
—JOY GOLLIVER

B elow is the Japanese symbol for Satori, which is a Japanese
Buddhist term for an instant awakening or sudden enlightenment.

When I read that Stephen Covey had died and I realized how one man had changed so many people's lives for the better, I had a satori. It was at that moment that I decided to share through this book all the research and knowledge I had accumulated on happiness.

A man named Saul was a persecutor and murderer of Christians. On the road to Damascus he had his satori and he became Paul. Saint Paul went on to write two-thirds of the New Testament of the Bible. Have you had a satori? You will never forget it when it comes.

Another satori came the next day at Stanford Alumni weekend. My friend Dr. Fred Luskin, PhD, had invited me to hear him speak at Memorial Auditorium on Stanford's campus. I sat in the first row, on the aisle. I got there early so I could get a good seat. My purpose in life became more focused as Dr. Luskin was swarmed by people who wanted to know more about happiness after his fabulous one-hour talk on the subject concluded. People ran onto the stage to gain more wisdom. I saw that people need help getting happier.

What is your purpose in life? Have you ever thought about it before? Are you too busy with work, family, and friends even to consider it? Are you afraid that working at a full-time job doesn't give you the time to have one? A lot of people work jobs that leave them unfulfilled. They do it to pay the bills. If that is your case, consider changing professions to one that aligns with your purpose. If that is not feasible right now, execute your purpose in life part-time. It's okay to take baby steps. If your purpose in life is to make sure that people have enough to eat, volunteer at a local food bank or soup kitchen. If your purpose in life is to help children realize their full potential, volunteer at a family shelter or a read at a local school. Don't let your life pass by another day until you at least try to figure out what your purpose in life is.

Purpose plus progress equals happiness. P +P = H. If you have figured out your purpose, it is time to start actually putting it into practice. You must make progress in your purpose. When you are actually living your purpose by putting action behind it, you will have happiness chase you down, knock you over, and tickle you pink. You will be the happiest you have ever been in your life. You will consider yourself successful, regardless of what other people say or think. You won't need or heed their good opinion of you anyway. Robert G. Allen said, "Don't let the opinions of the average man sway you. Dream, and he thinks you're crazy. Succeed, and he thinks you're lucky. Acquire wealth, and he thinks you're greedy. Pay no attention. He simply doesn't understand." If you can ignore the noise, you will be one of the few people in life that wakes up every morning raring to start your day and fulfill your purpose.

Dr. Wayne Dyer, in an article that appeared on healyourlife.com, wrote, "You'll feel most on purpose when you're giving your life away by serving others. When you're giving to others, to your planet, and to your Source, you're being purposeful." I have always loved Dr. Dyer's wisdom and insight. He is spot on when it comes to purpose. You will find your purpose when you put others first.

Make sure that your purpose in life is not just to make a lot of money. I know some of the country's richest people. They are no different from anyone else. I have found that the poor dream of being rich, and the rich dream of being happy. The happiest people that I know have a purpose. The happiest, wealthiest people I know love to give. They don't just write checks. They volunteer. They get involved. They are on the boards of charities. So find your noble purpose too.

CHAPTER 14

KINDNESS

Kindness in words creates confidence. Kindness in thinking creates profoundness. Kindness in giving creates love.
—LAO TZU

Kindness is best described as an act of good behavior or concern for others. Kindness is a virtue. A virtue is a quality that is thought to be good. It's an important foundation of a moral person. Kindness is highly valued and sought after in all cultures, religions, and philosophies throughout the world.

Be kind to people. Think back on who the kind people were in your life. Now think about the mean people in your life. It's a lot easier to remember all the meanies, isn't it? Don't be on someone's meanie list. It's almost impossible to get off of it. I'm sorry I made you think of those people because it can change your emotional state for the worse, but I needed to make a point. Now, go back to your nice person list. Wouldn't it be great if someone was reading this book and when I asked them to think of kind people, they thought of you? If you are a consistently kind person, they will.

If someone from your kind list were in need of help, wouldn't you help them? There are going to be times in your life when you need help. I'm talking life-threatening, job-on-the-line, lose-your-house kind of help. If you have been kind to others, don't sweat it. You've got kindness currency.

Kindness currency can only be redeemed when you have made a deposit into the universal kindness bank. That's why you need to be kind to people. It's in *your* best interest. I actually don't think of it that way, but it's true. I really enjoy being a kind person and I don't look for return favors. I love to give. However, if you are the type of person always looking for a "what's in it for me?" there's a lot in it for you. If you haven't been taught this already, this is your time to load up on your kindness deposits. The great thing is you will have great fun and happiness practicing it.

There is a Native American story of an Indian chief who tells his tribe that there are two dogs inside his head. One is a white dog that is loving and kind. The other is a black dog that is terrible and evil. He tells the tribe gathered around the fire that the dogs are going to fight to the death. A brave asks, "Which one of them will win." The chief says, "The one I feed."

In all of our heads is a constant struggle between good and evil, impatience and kindness. Feed kindness to people. The world is in dire need of it, now more than ever. The good news is you will never run out of it. No matter what your circumstances, kindness doesn't cost a thing. A smile or some consideration to someone who needs it will make both of you richer.

Mark Twain wrote, "Kindness is the language which the deaf can hear and the blind can see." This is one of his most famous quotes. It has stood the test of time because it is so true. Mark Twain is one of America's most brilliant minds of any era.

Born Samuel Langhorne Clemens in Florida, Missouri, in 1835, he became a printer, militia member, miner, newspaper reporter, writer, and riverboat pilot. He was very well traveled for his era. His pen name came from his experience as a riverboat pilot. "Mark twain" is a river term that means two fathoms. At two fathoms, it is safe to navigate a boat. He published more than thirty books and numerous articles. This man knew life. If he took the time to address the importance of kindness, it is worth heeding.

There is a great saying that I have always identified with: "Practice random acts of kindness." Great things have come from this simple saying. You can try these in your everyday life and get a thrill from them:

- Hold the door open for a long line of people and smile.
- When you are driving, let another car trying to merge or turn go ahead of you.
- Pay the toll for the person behind you in traffic.
- Be generous with compliments.
- Drop off a box of cookies at your local police or fire department. They need and deserve the thanks!
- Give someone a hug.
- Thank your parents in a letter.
- Praise your boss. It's a thankless job.
- Make someone laugh. You'll laugh too!
- Give your seat to an elderly person or a pregnant woman. A pregnant woman should never have to stand, unless she wants to.

Be kind to yourself. At the end of the day, you are the one person responsible for your happiness. If you are constantly being harsh to and berating yourself for perceived failures, you will never be happy. Although magnificent, you are not a perfect being. Accept this truth with kindness and self-love. Understand that you can learn from your mistakes and your flaws. Allow yourself to become a better person as a result of it.

Allow yourself some nurturing. We all need time alone. We all need to treat ourselves every once in a while. Do something that you love. Sneak away and see a movie at lunch. Work out. Take a walk and listen to your favorite music. Treat yourself to some new music. Get a massage and meditate during it. Just don't gorge yourself on bad food.

One of the most unkind things you can do to yourself is compare yourself to others. That is a recipe for disaster. We were all made differently and have different strengths, weaknesses, and gifts. We all have a place in this world that is necessary. You have one too. Just because your place is different from someone else's, doesn't mean it is not important.

When you flip the light switch at home, a light comes on. This is a result of many people with gifts different from yours (unless you are an electrician!). There are electricians that have the gift of wiring your house to the grid. There are accountants that have the gift of accurately organizing your account at the power company. There are engineers that have the gift of running the complex power grid itself. There are brave coal miners that have the gift of not freaking out that they are three miles below the earth in dangerous coal mines that supply the coal to run the power plant. There are farmers that have the gift of producing giant harvests from tiny seeds. They keep all of these people fed. There are doctors that have the gift of healing. They help keep all of these people well, so when you flip the light switch, a light comes on without you even thinking about it. There is no one more important than the other in this example. We are all integral and important.

When you compare yourself to others, it produces jealousy and envy within. These are extremely limiting emotions. You cannot pursue your purpose in life with a heart full of envy and self-doubt. Focus on what your gifts are. Strengthen those gifts. Develop those gifts to their maximum outcome. Are you athletic? Volunteer as a coach. Are you a good cook? Teach a cooking class. You'll have a blast doing what you love. Are you good with computers? Develop an app that helps people. Don't mope around the house, regretting that when you were little you were picked last on the playground. Super-successful, high-tech geniuses don't have time to waste thinking about how their gift was not something else. They are too busy changing the world for the better, using the gifts they were given.

There will always be people that have more money than you and less money than you. You will never be able to be the richest person on earth and stay at that post. The pursuit of material possessions will never make you happy anyway. Look at children the day after Christmas. They are bored with the toys that made them so excited the day before.

The pursuit of happiness will make you happy. Why? The pursuit of happiness, if you have assigned the right goals, is noble. True happiness is helping others with their pursuit as well. True happiness includes kindness to yourself and others.

Imagine that you are your best friend. Would you treat your best friend with continuous scorn and condemnation? Of course not! Treat yourself like you would treat your best friend because you are your best friend. Say kind words to yourself. Compliment yourself. Make a kindness list. Fill it with your best attributes. Make another list of how you have been kind to others. Is this list short? Make a list of things that you will do to be kind to others. You can use my random acts list for some ideas.

A lot of people strive to be perfect. They are easily disappointed in themselves, even though they have achieved significant outcomes. It is important to do your best. It is important to learn and grow more skilled. It is impossible to be perfect. You are just setting yourself up for failure if your desire is perfection. Love yourself and your imperfections. Believe in yourself. You'll always be able to accomplish more than you think you can.

CHAPTER 15

DON'T BE AFRAID!

Always do what you are afraid to do.
—Ralph Waldo Emerson

Fear can literally kill you. Fear is an incredibly destructive force in the human psyche. Fear comes from the Latin word *periculum*, which means "peril." Most people never become successful because they are afraid to fail. They are afraid to try because they fear what other people will say about them. One of the most frequent phrases in the Bible is "Do not be afraid." It is there for a reason. You can never accomplish your goals or be happy if you give in to fear.

As you go through your day, imagine you have an impenetrable shield in your left hand. Use that shield as protection against rejection, worry, and doubt. Lift up your shield and fend off negative comments, disillusionment, and disappointment. Avoid negative people. Avoid people that criticize you. Don't let anything hurt you or keep you down. The only time you should see fear is in your rear-view mirror. Fear is a choice.

In order to start an Up Cycle, which I define as a set of positive behaviors that lead to a positive outcome, you have to put your fear aside and believe that you can accomplish anything. You cannot make progress if you believe you cannot do it. Progress contributes to happiness. One of the most powerful motivators is accountability. I was able to lose weight and write this book, because I told over a hundred people what my goals were. If I were afraid to be accountable to my goals, you would be reading something else right now. Abandoning fear and embracing your true potential is an act that must occur daily. Ask yourself, "What's the worst that could happen if I decide to get healthy today? What's the worst that could happen if I decide to be happy right now?" Asking questions like these can remove your fear and turn your day in the right way.

I bid on a San Jose Sharks luxury box for a charity auction for my daughter's school, St. Charles. I won. During the game, I had the opportunity to spend some time with two-time Olympic hockey gold medalist Owen Nolan. He was part of the luxury-box package. What an incredibly nice and down to earth man he is. I asked him how he was so successful when the whole world was watching him. I asked him if he had a mantra or a ritual in order to block out the fear. He shook his head and said, "No, I just did my job. I had a job to do and I just focused on it."

That's what you must do every day. You must focus on the task at hand. Don't focus on the perceived enormity of the task. Few of us will ever be playing for a gold medal for our country and with a billion or so people watching. Clear the clutter and the mental chatter in your head. Nothing is ever as bad or as super complex as we make it out to be. Fear is just distracting chatter in a loop in your consciousness. It is completely unproductive. Never give into fear. It is the precursor to defeat.

Steve Jobs once said, "Remembering that I'll be dead soon is the most important tool I've ever encountered to help me make the big choices in life. Because almost everything—all external expectations, all pride, all fear of embarrassment or failure—these things just fall away in the face of death, leaving only what is truly important."

I am so glad he felt this way! He created revolutionary products that changed the way millions of people do business and communicate. His hard work created millions of jobs both directly and indirectly around the globe. He certainly had the right last name. His creations spurred industry and shrank the world. I am at the Apple campus in Cupertino quarterly for meetings. The people that I know there have not only been enriched financially, they have also flourished in their careers. They were given the opportunity to use their great educations and their imagination to create a better world.

Steve Jobs was abandoned by his biological birth parents and given up for adoption. Strike one. He never got a college degree. Strike two. He was even pushed out of Apple in 1985, the company that he started. Strike three. He never gave in to fear, however.

He started NeXT computer with $7 million in 1985. He almost ran out of money. He enlisted the help of Ross Perot. Perot invested in the company and Jobs turned a failure into a giant winner. Eleven years later, Jobs sold NeXT computer to, of all companies, Apple, for over $400 million. He became the CEO of Apple as well. Talk about returning as the conquering hero!

In addition to his work at Apple, in 1986, Jobs bought the Graphics Group from Lucasfilm for $10 million. It was later renamed Pixar. Pixar produced such hits as: *Toy Story, Toy Story 2, Toy Story 3, Monsters Inc., Finding Nemo, The Incredibles, Cars, Cars 2, A Bug's Life, Ratatouille, Wall-E,* and *Up.* All these movies were thoroughly enjoyable, wholesome family fare. In 2006, Disney bought Pixar for over $7 billion. That is an increase of seven hundred times the original investment, not to mention all the smiles, memories, and happiness Steve Jobs created.

When Steve jobs died on October 5, 2011, there was a pall over Silicon Valley. Most people in the Bay Area felt like they had lost a friend. I remember being drawn to the Apple store in Palo Alto, near where he lived. People were crying and leaving notes that they taped to the outside of the store. People were speechless that such a great man had been taken so early. He had a net worth estimated to be over $8 billion. Not bad for a college dropout. He was this generation's Thomas Edison. He was a bold, risk-taking entrepreneur. He was not afraid of failure and neither should you be.

Think about the great heroes in history. George Washington gave up a life of privilege and ease to endure terrible hardship and horrible living conditions to free America from foreign rule. He faced fear and was surrounded by death every day. Men died from the brutal winters alone. He did not give in to fear and became victorious. His sacrifice paved the way for generations to come. Because of his great sacrifice and the sacrifices of others, we have the United States of America.

Another hero was Joan of Arc. If there was ever a brave soul placed on this earth, it was Joan of Arc. She once said, "I am not afraid...I was born to do this." She led the French armies into many victories in the Hundred Years' War.

She was born a peasant girl around 1412, in the currently named French province of Lorraine. She beseeched Charles VII to let her don armor and lead the last vestiges of his troops into battle. For a generation, this army had been able to achieve on only a few victories. This was Charles's last hope. Joan of Arc immediately inspired the troops to take aggressive action and attack their foes, reclaiming much lost territory. Her decisive and bold strategies turned the tide and led to Charles VII ascension to the throne. She was eventually captured.

While in captivity, she made a daring escape. She jumped from a tower onto the ground from a height of seventy feet. She was recaptured and eventually burned at the stake. During her trial, she never expressed regret for her daring adventures and battles. The works of Shakespeare, Voltaire, Verdi, and George Bernard Shaw have immortalized her. To this day, politicians and scholars in every country often cite her heroism in the face of adversity.

When you start to become afraid, focus your thoughts on happy, fun emotions. My four-year-old son was very sick with a bad stomach virus. He had been vomiting for three days straight. It was two in the morning and he had woken up complaining he was going to puke. I held his little shaking body in front of the toilet. His body was uncontrollably convulsing and he was screaming in pain and terror. I wish I could have switched places with him. He was very scared.

I decided to help him out the best way I could. I told him to think about his favorite, fun times with his best friend, Seamus. I told him to think about sitting in the sandbox at preschool and to remember how the cool sand felt as he and Seamus built a sand castle with a funny little yellow bulldozer. I told him to remember how much fun it was to be with his best friend, laughing in the warm sunshine. I then told him that when he woke up later, we would be at a really fun party with Seamus and two other friends.

He immediately stopped shaking uncontrollably and stopped vomiting. He went back to bed and he didn't throw up again. I am convinced that by changing his thoughts from pain and fear to joy and pleasure, his body followed his mind. The change was miraculous and very relieving for the both of us. I will never forget that instantaneous change. It was a revelation.

Our thoughts control our emotions and our emotions control our reality. Here is an example: If someone tells you at work that they think you are going to lose your job, you probably go into a state of panic and fear immediately. That person could be wrong. They may have misread the situation. The reality might be that your job security is just fine. Your body and your emotions, however, become crippled with unnecessary fear. You start snapping at people, stop working so hard, and become ineffectual at your job. As a result of your negative thoughts about losing your job, you get fired because your negative thoughts effected your emotions, which changed your reality for the worse. That's another reason that you should never give in to fearful thoughts. Fearful thoughts do not produce positive outcomes.

Think about all the fears you have had during your life. Look back and see that, no matter what happened to you, you made it through. You are still alive. You are able to read or listen to this book. As you look ahead to your life, use your past to reassure yourself that you will overcome whatever comes your way. You have done it before. You *can* do it again. Don't let your fears trap you into a life of mediocrity. The choice has always been and will always be yours. Grab life by the horns, slay your fears, and be happy.

Can you imagine walking on a rope between the twin towers of the World Trade Center when they were standing? How about doing this without permission? Philippe Petit did this on August 7, 1974. The academy award–winning documentary, *Man on Wire*, chronicles this great feat. It was called the artistic crime of the century. I certainly am not condoning illegal activity. I am simply highlighting this man's bravery and his ability to dream and achieve the impossible.

When Petit heard about the plans to build the towers in New York City, he spoke to his friend about his dream to traverse them. He told his friend, "It's impossible, that's sure. So let's start working. If I die, what a beautiful death!" He planned the stunt for over a year. He snuck up to the roof just before the work was completed. He hid from patrolling policemen overnight. He shot an arrow attached to a guide wire to his coconspirator on the other tower in the cold darkness. They quickly strung the wire. Petit left the safety of the 110-story building and walked into the void.

The wire swayed up and down and side to side. It slumped in the middle and twisted. It felt as cold as ice as it rotated beneath his feet. Crowds gathered beneath. They screamed up to him. He waved. He danced. He lay down on the wire as the wind blew him back and forth. He celebrated life on the wire 1,100 above Manhattan for nearly an hour.

On each tower, the police waited to arrest him. A TV reporter interviewed one of the arresting officers, Sargent Charles Daniels. The officer said, "I observed the tightrope dancer...because you couldn't call him a walker...approximately halfway between the two towers. I personally figured I was watching something that somebody else would never see again in the world. Thought it was once in a lifetime."

Petit was arrested when he reached the other tower. He passed a psychological evaluation at a hospital and was brought to jail. He was released and didn't have to spend any more time in jail. Summing up his experience, he said, "Life should be lived on the edge of life. You have to exercise rebellion: to refuse to tape yourself to rules, to refuse your own success, to refuse to repeat yourself, to see every day, every year, every idea as a true challenge—and then you are going to live your life on a tightrope."

Philippe Petit went on to other daring high-wire walks. He even walked on a tightrope high above the city of Jerusalem. He recounts this hilarious and inspiring story in his TED talk, "The Journey across the High Wire." I encourage you to take the time to watch this fantastic eighteen-minute talk.

Man on Wire is one of my favorite movies. I had a personal connection to the twin towers. My father was the foreman during the construction of the restaurant, Windows on the World. It was located on the 106th and 107th floors of 1 World Trade Center. He took us there when it was completed in April of 1976. I was so proud of my dad's accomplishment. It was such a beautiful restaurant. It was mind-boggling to be up so high above the greatest city in the world and see so far. People that ate there never forgot its majestic elegance and heavenly views.

Philippe Petit, in his book *To Reach the Clouds: My High Wire Walk Between the Twin Towers*, wrote, "When the towers again twin-tickle the clouds, I offer to walk again, to be the expression of the builder's collective voice. Together, we will rejoice in an aerial song of victory. I will carry my life across the wire, as your life, as all our lives, past, present, and future—the lives lost, the lives welcomed since. We can overcome."

One way to not give into fear is to practice calmness. Be prepared for the waves to rock your small skiff that you call your life. After one wave passes, another will come, then another. Understand that life is a series of waves that shapes who we are. It is these challenges to our balance that will make us stronger and better able to deal with future imbalances. Learn how others kept their balance in difficult waters by reading and asking fellow captains what they did when all seemed lost. Wisdom comes from learning from our mistakes. A wise man learns from the mistakes of others.

Being calm in the face of a storm takes discipline. You must focus on being calm. You cannot let your oar falling into the sea rattle you. If you only have one oar left, make the best of it. Use that one oar to methodically and precisely get you to a new oar or, better yet, get you to a new yacht. If you retain your focus and practice inner peace, you can make the best of any situation. There are times that you must see yourself as a massive rock, or a mighty oak tree planted beside the water. You shall not be moved.

Then there are times that you must envision yourself like an Olympic gymnast on the balance beam. You twist, leap, bend over backward, and do a summersault. You can do whatever it takes to achieve victory without falling down. If a fourteen-year-old gymnast can do these routines flawlessly with the entire world watching, you can get through your workday with peace and dignity, if you focus your thoughts on being calm in the face of adversity.

When I am in my car, alone, I often do not turn on the radio. I have learned that I don't always have to fill my head with the world's stimuli. It is a great time to be alone with my thoughts. I use the time to plan how I am going to tackle the rest of the day in the most productive way. I ask myself questions like: "How can I be a better husband to my wife and a better father to my children? What can I say to them that will let them know how much I love and appreciate them? What activities can we do as a family that will create a great memory that we can all enjoy for the rest of our lives?"

In a calm state, I open up and let the answers come to me. They always do. When you are in a state of peace, the best thoughts and solutions come. When you are in a frenetic state, that's when you find yourself starving for answers and thirsty for knowledge that doesn't come as often or as clearly.

CHAPTER 16

NO MORE EXCUSES

Never give up. Never give in. Never, Never, Never!
—Sir Winston Churchill

Are you happy? The good news is that happiness is a choice. I will show you the steps to break free from the chains of depression. The choice is yours. You just have to make the decision to be happy from NOW on.

Most people worry about money. Worrying and happiness do not co-exist well. In the United States more people are more afraid of dying broke than actually dying!

My mother died of cancer when I was seventeen years old. I was very close to her and it turned my world upside down. I became unhappy. I understand that you are in whatever stage of emotional being in your life through myriad complex reasons and certain psychological traumas as well. Don't let your past control your present. The past is gone. Forgive yourself. Forgive the people that have hurt you. I know it's easier said than done, but that forgiveness will be a present to yourself. It is one of the best gifts you can give yourself. Mark Twain said, "Anger is an acid that can do more harm to the vessel in which it is stored than to anything on which it is poured." All that matters is what we make of today and how we set ourselves up for tomorrow. We all face disappointments. We all suffer loss. How we handle it is what makes us, us.

I get my love of food from my mother. My mother was a chef for a two ultra high-end catering firms in Manhattan. She met and cooked for President Ronald Reagan, Senator Jay Rockefeller, Senator Daniel Patrick Moynihan (who nominated my sister to attend Kings Point Merchant Marine Academy), and several mayors of New York including Abe Beam, David Dinkins, and Ed Koch. I actually worked as a bartender for Mayor Koch when I was seventeen, at Gracie mansion. He was a truly colorful character. My mother cooked for many other famous people, including Elizabeth Taylor, Jackie O., Richard Harris, Jackie Gleason, and Richard Burton. She catered parties at such unique places as the Metropolitan Museum of Art, the Guggenheim, and Tiffany's.

She was an incredible cook, and such a hard worker. When she was eight months' pregnant with my sister Catherine, she was cooking for a big gala event and fainted from the heat. When she recovered, she went back to cooking for four hours and then took the train home by herself at 1:00 in the morning. She wouldn't call my dad to pick her up. She was an incredibly strong, kind, and happy person. Everybody loved her. Nothing and no one could stop her. Unfortunately, cancer did. I still love her and miss her very much, but I am so very grateful that I had seventeen years with her.

She taught me all about cooking. When I was twelve, she started buying me *The Good Cook* series from Time-Life. Every few months, I would get a new book in the mail. I was eager to try the recipes when the book came. One book was just for fish. I made fish until we all had scales. One book was just for poultry. I made every chicken dish under the sun. She would let me cook dinner for the family under her watchful eye. While I cooked, my mother would be talking on the white kitchen wall phone that had a twenty-foot cord.

It seemed like she was always on that phone. Somehow she managed to vacuum our entire fifty-foot-long house while on the phone with only a twenty-foot phone cord, and smoking a non-filter Pall Mall cigarette.

The phone was always ringing. You *always* answered it. At three years old, children were taught to answer the phone. There was no such thing as voicemail to hide behind. Back then, neighbors just dropped by unannounced for a drink and a smoke. They would stay for dinner. I poured Jameson Irish whiskey, Harvey's Bristol Cream, and Lancer's white wine and fetched Schaeffer beers in between rolling out the dough for a beef Wellington. I emptied and cleaned heavy leaded-glass ashtrays until they shined, while waiting for the pasta to drain. The enormous, remote-less, fake-wood console TV was always on. Merv Griffin, Donny and Marie, the Muppets, and Walter Cronkite were part of the family. I remember the lemon-yellow Sears stove and our awful avocado-green refrigerator. It was '70s home decor at its finest. Throw in Joe Namath, the Summer of Sam, Rockaway Beach, the N train, football in the street, and Gino's pizza and that was my childhood growing up in New York City. But boy, can I cook!

I wrote this book for a number of reasons. The first and most important reason was to help people. I truly love people. Nothing makes me happier than when I help someone. I also love when people succeed. This is my passion. I am not jealous of other people's successes. When I see someone succeed, I am genuinely happy for them. I also know that I can succeed as well, because they did. I met some incredible mentors that shared with me secrets and technology for achieving goals. I have to put out my story so others can benefit from these techniques.

I want you to have the greatest, most positive life possible. Try to read more books and articles on the subject of happiness.

Attended seminars. When you are in your car, listen to positive authors on CD. More importantly, implement the knowledge that you receive. Happiness is a **skill** that must be learned, sharpened, practiced, shared, and used.

I also wrote this book for my two children and their children. I won't be around forever. I'll never be able to tell them verbally all that I have learned in my life. This is one father's life manual for his beloved children. I am truly blessed to be the father of Kendall and Michael Duffy. I have never known joy the way I feel it as a parent. It is my responsibility on this earth to prepare my children for all that life has to throw at them. I don't take that responsibility lightly. It is my highest calling. As I write these words, I am speaking directly to them. It is my love for them that drives me to complete this work. I see great things for these two wonderful people. Watch out world, here they come.

One day at a Cuban restaurant in Palo Alto, I picked up a copy of the *Wall Street Journal* and saw that Stephen Covey had died. His *7 Habits of Highly Successful People* was groundbreaking and had a big influence on my life. Right then, I decided to write this book. I asked the waitress to get me a pen and some paper, and I started writing out chapter titles.

I walked into a party four hours later and told everyone at the party I was going to write this book. The look of disbelief on a lot of people's faces that I would claim publicly that I would write a book while still working full-time was funny to me. I knew I could do it because I was using the principle of accountability. I had purposely applied pressure on myself, something most people do their best to avoid. But coal doesn't become a diamond sitting on the couch. It takes immense pressure to create something beautiful.

CHAPTER 17

POWER FOODS

> *No disease that can be treated by diet should*
> *be treated with any other means.*
> —Maimonides

There are foods that are more powerful and beneficial than pharmaceutical drugs when it comes to your health and happiness. You don't hear in the media about people giving up their medications for high blood pressure, asthma, and arthritis by eating healthier because there is no money in it. Some of these foods are old-fashioned grandma and grandpa foods that we think of today as passé or quaint. Oatmeal is an example.

Oatmeal in the morning is one of the greatest things you could possibly eat to start off your day. Oats contain zinc, selenium, copper, manganese, vitamin E, magnesium, and iron. Oats have been shown to be a good cancer-fighting food. Studies have shown that people that eat oats have a lower chance of heart disease. The U.S. Food and Drug Administration allows oatmeal producers to put a label on their products that oatmeal may reduce the risk of heart disease when combined with a low-fat diet. The American Diabetes Association endorses oats as a food that can help control glucose levels in the blood. Oats are a good source of protein. Oatmeal helps you feel full longer, which staves off those pre-lunch hunger pangs.

Try adding a tablespoon of freshly ground organic flaxseed to a half cup of organic rolled outs. In a coffee grinder, grind only enough flaxseed to last you a week. Store the meal in the refrigerator in a tightly sealed container. Flaxseed contains omega-3 fatty acids, which help reduce the risk of blood clots. People with heart disease are encouraged to take flaxseed. As it also helps reduce inflammation in the body, people with asthma and arthritis are encouraged to take flaxseed. Flaxseed is high in fiber, which has been shown to reduce the "bad" cholesterol. It stabilizes blood sugar. It contains magnesium, which helps reduce blood pressure. King Charlemagne of France believed so strongly in the health benefits of flaxseed, he required his subjects to eat it. Flaxseed contains lignans, which are powerful antioxidants. Flaxseed contains more lignans than other plant foods. It is a superfood that you cannot pass up. You only have one life. If you treat your body right by eating the right foods like these superfoods, you will live longer, stronger, and happier.

Try adding about a cup of unsweetened organic almond milk to the oatmeal and flaxseed. Almond milk is fantastic. It tastes so much better than making oatmeal with hot water. Having the creamy flavor and texture of almond milk instead of water in your oatmeal increases the enjoyment of your breakfast experience. The protein molecules in almond milk are smaller and easier to digest. It has a very pleasant flavor. Unsweetened almond milk has only 40 calories per eight-ounce serving. It has fewer calories than dairy milk and soymilk. It contains vitamins A, D, E, magnesium, phosphorous, 150 mg of potassium, and 300 mg of calcium. It has 0 grams of saturated fat. It is a low sodium and low glycemic food. It is packed with antioxidants, which increases the body's immunity to disease. The calcium protects against bone diseases such as osteoporosis and helps give you strong teeth. The vitamin A aids your eyesight.

Put all of this in a Tupperware container and seal it with a lid. Store in the refrigerator overnight. You can make three days' worth of oatmeal at a time. In the morning, you can add raisins and fresh fruit. Popular favorites are blueberries, strawberries, bananas, pomegranate seeds, cherries, raspberries, and blackberries. That's the beauty of oatmeal. It is a blank palette that you can add color and flavor to. It will power you through your morning.

I invented a Happiness Cocktail that you can take every morning before you eat your breakfast. It can replace your morning sugary coffee. A lot of Americans look forward to the fall for two reasons: football and pumpkin spice lattes. My Happiness Cocktail consists of four awesome, life-improving ingredients:

> 4 ounces of organic wheat grass, fresh or frozen
> 1 tablespoon of Carlson lemon-flavored cod liver oil
> 1 tablespoon of organic chia seeds
> The juice of half an organic lemon

Take all the ingredients, put in a glass and stir vigorously. Put a few 50/50 spirulina and chlorella tablets in your mouth. Wash down the tablets with my Happiness Cocktail.

Wheat grass is a superfood. It has more than ninety different minerals in it. It is one of the most nutrient-dense foods on the planet. Wheatgrass restores alkalinity, detoxifies, and helps your blood and liver. It helps your skin look better. It increases your energy. It is high in protein. It helps stave off cancer. It boosts your immune system. It aids digestion. It helps you lose weight. I either juice it myself or buy it in frozen ice cubes from an organic farmer in Canada. He grows it outdoors. He ships it in dry ice. It is convenient to buy it this way because you don't have to clean your juicer every day.

Cod liver oil is high in docosahexaenoic acid. DHA is an omega-3 fatty acid that is great for your nervous system. Americans have been reporting increasing levels of depression. DHA can help treat and prevent depression. Cod liver oil also contains eicosapentaenoic acid, another omega-3. EPA decreases inflammation. If you suffer from arthritis or asthma, you should eat EPA-rich foods. EPA is high in vitamin A and D. Vitamin A is great for your eyesight and skin, and for digestive disorders. Vitamin D is necessary for strong bones and teeth, the regulation of blood pressure, blood sugar levels, and a healthy immune system. It helps prevent type 2 diabetes. (Note: refrigerate your bottle of cod liver oil after opening.)

Chia seeds are not just for Chia Pets anymore! They are a unique food. Chia is similar in nutritional value to flaxseed, but doesn't have to be ground in order to be digested. Chia seeds look like tiny poppy seeds. When exposed to water, they begin to increase in size and start to gel. That gelling action will make your stomach feel full. Like cod liver oil, they are rich in omega-3 fatty acids. If you are a vegetarian and don't eat fish, you should add chia seeds to your diet. Chia seeds are also full of soluble and insoluble fiber. Your body needs fiber to ensure regularity. Fiber helps stave off diseases such as diverticulosis and diverticulitis. Chia seeds also help balance blood sugar, and lower the risk of type 2 diabetes. They also provide steady energy throughout the day. Chia seeds are rich in antioxidants. Would you like healthier, younger-looking skin, hair, and nails? Chia seeds are what the dermatologist ordered.

Lemon juice has been used medicinally for thousands of years. It is low in calories. Lemon juice is one of the best sources of vitamin C, which helps increase your immunity and is also great for the skin. It is high in potassium. Potassium lowers blood pressure, which can reduce the risk of heart disease. Most people think that lemon juice is acidic, but it is actually alkaline. Lemon juice aids digestion and stimulates your gallbladder to release the previous day's stored toxins. It kills the parasites in your body and your mouth, and aids in kidney and liver function.

Spirulina and chlorella are algae. They have been used as a supplement in Japan for many years. They have one of the highest concentrations of protein of any food you can buy. They have been described as the "perfect food." Chlorella contains vitamins B, C and E, iron, and zinc. These vitamins improve the immune system and aid in healing. Spirulina contains gamma-linolenic acid. GLA's are fatty acids, which contribute to hormonal balance. Spirulina and chlorella reduce inflammation in the joints and tissues. Because they are high in protein and low in calories, they can help reduce obesity and increase energy levels. The world's top athletes take this supplement to achieve peak performance. I like the tablet form. Do not chew the tablets because they do not taste good. The powders have a horrible aftertaste.

Avocado is an incredible superfood and a delicious addition to any meal. Avocados contain carotenoid lutein, which helps your vision. They are high in beta-sitosterol, a phytonutrient that lowers cholesterol. Avocados contain glutathione (an antioxidant), folate, and vitamin E, which helps your heart function correctly and lowers your chance of stroke. Some vitamins and other nutrients can only be dissolved in fat. The healthy fat that this fruit contains helps your body process these vital nutrients. Avocados have been shown to prevent oral cancer and prostate cancer. Their high concentration of oleic acid helps fight breast cancer.

When it comes to selecting the best foods to optimize your health, always opt for nutrient-dense foods. Avoid foods that are empty calories, such as candy or potato chips. Avocados are one of the most nutrient-dense foods on the planet. The average California (Haas) avocado has 200 calories. The larger Florida variety has 300 calories. I prefer the Haas variety. It is richer, creamier, and more flavorful. For this paltry 200 calories, you get all of the nutrients I've listed plus vitamin C, vitamin B, vitamin K, fiber, pantothenic acid, magnesium, potassium, riboflavin, and niacin. Replace milk and yogurt with avocado in your smoothies. It will provide a sweet, creamy rich texture. Instead of using mayonnaise or butter on your sandwich, use plain avocado or guacamole. Cut in slices or cubes and place on top of your salads. They really make a turkey sandwich taste much better.

My kids wouldn't eat spinach until I brought an iPad over to the table and introduced them to Popeye. You don't see Popeye on TV anymore. I grew up on Popeye. They loved the cartoon with its absurd artwork and silly voices. The theme of every episode of the cartoon is to eat your spinach and you will be able to accomplish anything. They couldn't wait to eat their spinach! Mikey and Kendall really believed that after dinner they were ten times stronger and had more energy. It was wonderful to see their imaginations at work. They were laughing, smiling, and happy as they ran around pretending to lift heavy imaginary items.

Spinach grows to about a foot in height. It is thought to have originated in Persia. Traders took it to India and then to China. Ever wonder why dishes with the word "Florentine" in them, like eggs Florentine, always have spinach in them? In 1533, Catherine de' Medici became queen of France. She loved spinach so much she insisted it be served at every meal. Because of this, meals made with spinach are known as Florentine, because of Catherine's birth in Florence, Italy.

Where do I start when it comes to the health effects of spinach? First of all, it is an excellent source of fiber. If you've ever cooked fresh spinach, you know that it reduces down to very little. What you are left with is an intensely dark, nutrient-dense, low-calorie, and delicious versatile vegetable. In raw form, it has only 23 calories per 100 grams. It is low in fat. It is a great diet food. It fills you up and curbs your appetite.

Feeling run down and anemic? Maybe you have an iron deficiency. 100 grams of uncooked spinach has 25 percent of the U.S. recommended daily allowance (RDA) of iron. Iron helps build red blood cells, which carry oxygen to our cells. Pound for pound, it has more iron than beef.

Spinach is loaded with vitamin K, which we need for strong bones and a healthy brain, myelin sheath, and other components of the nervous system. Vitamin K also helps guard against stroke and atherosclerosis. It contains beta-carotene and lutein for your eyes. Your heart benefits from its potassium. It has powerful antioxidants in vitamin C, zinc, vitamin E, manganese, and selenium, which help maintain proper blood pressure. For men, its flavonoids (phytonutrients) help stave off prostrate cancer.

The vitamin A in spinach is great for your skin, which helps you look younger. Vitamin A also helps boost immunity by creating white blood cells. One cup of spinach provides over 300 percent of the RDA of vitamin A.

Another power food is sunflower seeds. The sunflower plant is like today's most advanced solar panels. It actually follows the arc of the sun throughout the day, converting the sun's powerful rays into a perfect food. Native Americans had been using the sunflower for thousands of years when the Spanish Conquistadors brought it back to Spain. There it spread to the rest of Europe and Asia.

Sunflower oil is one of the most popular cooking oils in the world. The seeds can elevate your mood. The choline and tryptophan they contain can improve memory and reduce anxiety and depression. They are nature's antidepressants. Sunflower seeds are an incredibly nutrient-dense food, containing a variety of important vitamins, minerals, and antioxidants.

Instead of eating coffee cake, bagels, muffins, or donuts for breakfast, try my happiness cocktail or oatmeal. Don't believe, like most Americans, the seductive marketing campaigns and TV ads that their bad food will make you happy. Put sugary cereals forever in your rearview mirror. Don't miss out on living and eating healthy on purpose!

CHAPTER 18

THE DANGERS OF SUGAR

Would you get your dog up in the morning
with a cup of coffee and a donut?
—Jack LaLanne

Today, most processed foods contain some form of sugar, usually high fructose corn sugar or processed white sugar. Neither is a naturally occurring substance. It's like the difference between having a cup of coca leaf tea and snorting cocaine.

In South America, millions of people have coca leaf tea. It is not bad for you. However, if you take the leaves and chemically extract the cocaine and snort this highly concentrated powder, you can die. You may not die the first time you try cocaine, but over time, cocaine will ruin your mind and body. You won't die from eating a chocolate chip cookie, but if you overburden your body with these abnormal concentrations of sugar, it will ruin your body over time.

Many researchers have come to the conclusion that sugar is the primary factor in the obesity epidemic in the United States. In the 1970s and '80s, it was thought that if you ate fat, you became fat. This started the low-fat craze. Fat was taken out and sugar was put in to processed foods. Guess what? Obesity and diabetes skyrocketed.

A processed food may contain sugar, but the ingredient list on the label will not include that word. It will likely list "dextrose," which is just another name for sugar. The nutrition label also lists total carbohydrates and, below that, total sugars and fiber. The manufacturers can't disguise the sugars there.

A good rule of thumb that most doctors recommend is to eat less than 25 grams of sugar a day. Did you know that a serving of barbecue sauce has around 32 grams of sugar? Did you know that the low-fat chocolate milk you feed your kids has about 25 grams of sugar? But hey, it's milk and it's low fat! It has more sugar than one serving of Kool-Aid, which has about 16 grams of sugar.

Here are some of the terrible things that sugar has been linked to:

- Sugar can cause antisocial behavior in children. Studies have shown that crankiness and anxiety are elevated after ingestion. Symptoms of attention deficit disorder have been more acute as a result of sugar. Test scores and the ability to concentrate on tasks have been shown to decrease due to sugar.
- Studies have shown that inflammation can be caused by sugar. This inflammation can cause heart disease.
- Sugar increases acidity in the mouth. This can cause tooth decay and periodontal disease.
- Sugar can contribute to diabetes, gastric cancer, pancreatic cancer in women, heart disease, gallstones, Alzheimer's, gout, colon cancer, Parkinson's disease, and prostrate cancer.
- Sugar is an addictive substance. Dependence on any substance can lead to depression and hopelessness.

Given all the research that scientists have done on sugar, try to make a conscious effort to cut down on it. Research has shown that it takes three weeks to create a new habit. Try cutting out sugar, cold turkey, for three weeks. You'll be glad you did.

CHAPTER 19

EXERCISE

*Physical fitness is not only one of the most
important keys to a healthy body, it is the basis
of dynamic and creative intellectual activity.*
—JOHN F. KENNEDY

Exercise can help you get happier. Check with your doctor to
see if it is safe for you to exercise and ask what he or she would
recommend you do.

Working out changes your emotional state of mind. You forget
about all those problems and focus on the task at hand. It gives
your emotional mind a break. You actually get more energy by expending energy. When you are finished, you know you have accomplished something good. You can be proud of yourself. It is
important to be proud of yourself. Working out alleviates depression. It can break the cycle of negative, downward thinking.

You must be a person of action. I work with wealthy and successful people. The one thing that they all have in common is that they
are people of action. You don't become a CEO of a major tech company by being lazy. You don't become an Olympic athlete by watching *Cake Boss*. You don't want to get to the end of your life with
regrets. That is not a life well lived. That is a waste. You must fulfill

your potential and not be resentful and envious of others. Where will resentment get you? It will get you fatter.

I was having lunch one beautiful spring day at Google with a Google employee. The cherry blossoms on the campus were in full bloom. On our way back to my car, we ran into Sergey Brin. He was working out. They have a parallel bar on a dirt trail by a rustic creek on campus. He was shirtless and waiting for another employee to finish his reps on the bar. He recognized my friend and they exchanged pleasantries. First I thought, "Wow! This is one of the richest and most powerful men on the planet, talking to my friend. This is so cool!" Then I thought, "Man, Sergey Brin is ripped!"

Sergey Brin is the cofounder of Google. Forbes named him and his partner, Larry Page, as the fifth most powerful men in the world in 2009. He has an estimated net worth of over $20 billion.

Do not think that when everything works out, when you get rich, or when you can find the time, you will work out. Please do not also think, "Well, if I had $20 billion dollars, I would work out too!" What I learned from that chance encounter with Sergey Brin is that if you want to get in shape, no amount of money will actually push and pull your body up and down on a set of parallel bars. You have to exercise your body yourself. If Sergey Brin, with all of his commitments, time constraints, and enormous pressure, can find the time and the drive to work out, so can you!

Instead of taking out your frustrations on a bag of Fritos, go for a jog. Instead of eating (and you are not going to believe this, but it is true!) a cheeseburger with two frosted donuts as the bun, which they serve at Straw restaurant in San Francisco, walk. Instead of feeling sorry for yourself and huddling away from the world under a dark blue blanket on the couch, take that depressing blue blanket and stretch it from the couch to the chair and invite your kids into your fort. Use the coach cushions as walls and a door. Take pictures of your new castle and post your child peeking out from the "door" of the fort. Make a great memory instead of wallowing in depression. Choose happiness and motion over sadness and a sedentary lifestyle.

So what should you do? Do something! Plan to do formal exercise at least three times a week. There are two basic types of exercise: aerobic and anaerobic. Aerobic means "with oxygen." A higher percentage of fat is burned during aerobic exercise than during anaerobic exercise. Anaerobic means "without oxygen."

Aerobic exercise is the most popular type of exercise for losing weight. Typical aerobic exercises are jogging, cross-country skiing, Zumba, swimming, stair climbing, bicycling, and rowing. Aerobic exercise will elevate your mood. It lifts depression, reduces stress, reduces anxiety, and can help you sleep (because you will be tired!). It helps strengthen your heart and can reduce plaque buildup in your arteries. It helps the transport of lymph through your lymph system. Lymph is the fluid that circulates throughout that system, picking up bacteria and other harmful allergens and bringing them to lymph nodes where they are destroyed. The lymphatic system has no central pump, so exercise can facilitate the transport of this necessary fluid. Exercise also elevates your immune system to ward off colds.

Regular aerobic exercise can not only help you live longer, it can also help you live a happier life. Exercising releases endorphins in the brain. Endorphins are also released when you do dangerous recreational drugs or eat chocolate. Have you heard of a runner's high? You can also plug into groups that will increase your social life like a runners group or social outings at the gym. So you get more friends when you exercise too. It's great to associate with other people that share your interests. Last time I checked, there were no evening TV/ice cream groups starting up near my house.

Aerobic activity can reduce the likelihood of you developing heart disease, type 2 diabetes, high blood pressure, heart attack, stroke, and cancer. It improves bone density, lowering the chances of osteoporosis. A good diet and exercise is much better than taking medication for a lot of these conditions, plus they can help you avoid these health problems altogether. Proper nutrition and exercise can increase your stamina, reduce your health risks, and help you manage chronic conditions such as arthritis. Aerobic exercise improves balance. It helps give you the extra energy you need to do the activities of daily living like cleaning the house or playing with your kids. It increases your self-esteem.

Anaerobic exercise is high-intensity muscular activity that lasts for a short period of time. Examples of anaerobic exercise include weight lifting, calisthenics, and sprinting. Anaerobic exercise does not require large amounts of oxygen because the activity is brief.

Anaerobic exercise like weight lifting builds and maintains muscle. A sedentary lifestyle leads to a loss of muscle mass and strength. Lifting weights can speed your metabolism. It also builds bone strength. It prevents heart disease and lower back pain. It helps reshape your body and improve your appearance. A better-looking you is a happier you.

What are you waiting for? Get your Nikes on and go outside your door, now! Just don't go overboard and hurt yourself. Build up your stamina slowly. Rome and Arnold Schwarzenegger weren't built in a day. A lot of people do too much and then they get hurt and then they quit. Get an exercise buddy. Write down your achievements on your smartphone or a piece of paper. Try to increase your exercise in terms of both effort and duration. When you look back at where you started, you'll be amazed at your progress.

CHAPTER 20

REPLACE BAD HABITS

The only proper way to eliminate bad habits
is to replace them with good ones.
—JEROME HINES

I drink tea every morning. I used to drink coffee. Green tea is so good for you. Green teas include epigallocatechin gallate (EGCG) complex, an excellent antioxidant. Green tea contains only 5 to 10 percent of the caffeine in a cup of coffee and it boosts your immune system. The jasmine flowers in this tea blend bring some sweetness and spice to an otherwise boring flavor profile, at least for me.

I discovered a whole world of tea that was already there, but I didn't see it. There are teahouses devoted entirely to tea. Tea is the second most consumed beverage in the world after water. There are different kinds of tea. There is white, green, black, rooibos, mate, herbal, and oolong. Tea is a great, calorie-free way to increase your water intake and satisfy cravings.

I replaced a lot of my TV watching with writing and researching. I love to go to the library. I am all business there. If I am going to take the time to go to the library, I am going to write or read all the pertinent books that apply to my current topic. The library is awesome. I am grateful to be surrounded by wonderful libraries on the Peninsula, which is just south of San Francisco. The local governments have spent enormous amounts of money to make them beautiful and filled with knowledge. They have the most up-to-date books on everything. If they don't have a book, they will order it. My wonderful dad taught me this. He reads a book a week. He gets them from his local library in Connecticut. If you haven't been to a library in years, stop by one. It's much better than a coffee shop. Most let you bring in your beverage now as well. For me, a hot cup of tea, a full battery on my MacBook and I am ready to rock and roll.

I made a conscious decision to examine my life and the time that I spend and turn bad behaviors into lifelong productive behaviors. I sat down and made a list of how I spend my time. On one side of the page I wrote old, bad behaviors. On the other side of the page, I wrote new replacement behaviors. It looks like this:

Old, Bad Behaviors	New Replacement Behaviors
Watching too much TV.	Limiting TV to one hour a day. Researching and writing books.
No established date nights.	Saturday night is date night.
Mindless surfing of the Internet.	Limiting internet surfing to thirty minutes per day.
Talking on the phone too long.	Limiting calls to an average of 10 minutes per call.
Not prioritizing my workday.	Establishing a schedule at work.
Letting life goals go by the wayside.	Establishing a happiness partner.

Replace talking endlessly about unimportant things with your friends and call your happiness partner. A happiness partner is a friend or family member that you share your happiness goals with. Do you want to ride a horse or learn ballroom dancing? Tell your happiness partner whatever your goals are. Tell them when you will have this done. Try to make the deadline within a week. Have them share with you what they want to do. Check back in a week to see if they did it. You are accountable to your partner. Don't let them down.

Do this exercise of writing down a list of your bad behaviors and your replacement behaviors. You will be surprised at how different and more fulfilling your life will become. If you have children, you will become a great role model for them. When your children know that you are at the library and not at the bar, what kind of choices do you think they will make in life? When they see you state your goals and achieve them, they are more likely to model your behavior as well. If you don't have kids, you will inspire your family, friends, and coworkers.

Fill in the table on the next page with behaviors that you would like to change.

Old, Bad Behaviors	New Replacement Behaviors

CHAPTER 21

DECISIONS VS. WISHES

You cannot make progress without making decisions.
—JIM ROHN

You have to make a decision to be happy. Do not make a wish. When you make a happiness decision, make it binding. You are going to do everything in your power to achieve and maintain your happiness goal. Like a smoker who will never light up again, so too you must maintain your happiness habits forever. You have to have a lifetime resolve of choosing happiness on this journey.

Maintenance is just as important as the initial dedication phase. If you wanted to lose weight, you have to ignore junk food like Cool Ranch Doritos. (Where is that cool ranch anyway? It sounds like such a cool place to visit!) You have to pay attention to everything that you put in your mouth. You have to have a goal weight and measure your weight every day. You have to make a decision to stay at that goal weight and do whatever is necessary to accomplish it. That means sacrifice.

Every meaningful thing in life requires sacrifice. Instant gratification leads to eventual pain. If you want to have good grades, you have to study and sacrifice watching TV and partying with your friends. If you want to have a happy marriage, you have to be willing to sacrifice and let your spouse do the things they want to do.

You have to sacrifice the instant gratification of telling someone off. Yelling at someone usually leads to regret. Sacrificing the need to be right with the need to be happy is a better choice.

The great news is that you get rewarded for your sacrifice! It is difficult for the present you to understand this. You have to take it on faith. Hard work always pays off. The future-you will be so grateful for the sacrifice the present-you is making.

The best analogy I can use to show the difference between a decision and a wish is painting a room. When you paint a room, you finish painting the room. You do not paint half the room and give up. You would not even consider painting half the room. That is because you made a decision to paint the room. If people came to your house and saw one wall painted three-quarters white and one-quarter pink, they would be confused and ask you what happened. So should it be with your happiness. Stay committed to being happy no matter what happens in your life. Keep your cool and be grateful for everything that comes your way.

Would you paint a room and then dip your hands in liquid chocolate and make handprints on your freshly painted walls? Of course you would not. If marks did appear on your new walls, you would strenuously wipe them clean until they were gone. If you start to get depressed, you must do the same thing. You must be vigilant to maintain your sparkling new happy attitude.

CHAPTER 22

BE ENTHUSIASTIC!

*Enthusiasm is the yeast that makes your hopes shine
to the stars. Enthusiasm is the sparkle in your eyes, the
swing in your gait. The grip of your hand, the irresistible
surge of will and energy to execute your ideas.*
—Henry Ford

Always be enthusiastic. Enthusiasm brings up everyone around you. At work, being enthusiastic can help increase morale and productivity. At home, it can inspire your spouse and your kids to participate in family activities. The TV is the enemy of family activities. Enthusiasm helps cajole your kids to put down the remote. Enthusiasm is the energy that fuels success. Vince Lombardi once said, "If you aren't fired with enthusiasm, you will be fired with enthusiasm." Take it from one the greatest football coaches of all time, the working world has little time for goldbrickers.

Enthusiasm makes life more enjoyable. It helps you be a more effective communicator. You may speak a different language from someone, but you can still tell that the person you can't understand is enthusiastic. It is a universal form of positive communication. When you are enthusiastic, people will find you and your message more attractive. It will incite you and whomever you are trying to influence into taking action.

Enthusiasm is a skill just like happiness. There will be times when you won't have any enthusiasm. That's when you have to sharpen your skill. You have to reach deep inside and make a conscious effort to stay engaged. When you have run out of enthusiasm, act like you are enthusiastic. Smile and become active. Get out of your chair and jump up and down. Think of something funny to change your emotions. Keep something that makes you laugh on your smartphone or computer and watch it during these lethargic bouts.

Make sure you are getting enough sleep and enough exercise. A good diet will help keep your enthusiasm up as well. If you are overeating, you will feel tired. If you are not drinking enough water, that can work against you too. Make sure you are hydrated to stay in peak, sunshine form.

Focus on what you are passionate about. If you love your career, like I do, you will race into the office and can't wait to get started. When you love what you do, enthusiasm just shows up. If you hate your job, your enthusiasm will dissipate. If that is the case, it is time to go.

In bicycle racing, people line up behind the leader. It's called drafting. When you have someone expending the energy to break the headwind, it makes it easier on you. You can also do this with enthusiasm. Find someone in your office who is enthusiastic. Spend some time with them. You can catch their contagious positive energy. That will set you up for the sprint toward the rest of the day.

Get inspirational CDs or books on your phone and listen to them when you are in the car, at the gym, or at home. Inspirational books can help you overcome and achieve your goals. You will have a powerful subconscious loop in your head that you can do anything. It's the truth.

Tune out negative media. We live in a skeptical, complaining society. Tragedy, apathy, and disappointment rule the mainstream news cycle. Preprogram the media that you will consume. Don't let the bad news consume you. Make sure what you watch will elevate you to an enjoyable higher level of thinking.

The word "enthusiasm" comes from the Greek *enthousiasmos,* which means to be inspired. Consistently enthusiastic people are a force to be reckoned with. People are attracted to them. They are usually very successful individuals. Why? They are focused on a goal. They will not be stopped, no matter how many hurdles pop up in front of them. Dale Carnegie said, "Flaming enthusiasm, backed up by horse sense and persistence, is the quality that most frequently makes for success."

The most enthusiastic person I know is my friend Dalena. She followed her dream and started a modeling business. When she told me that she was leaving her job, I encouraged her to go. I knew that, whatever she put her mind to, she was going to be a success. Sure enough, today she runs an incredibly successful and profitable business. She is so happy that she left her job to pursue her dream of helping other people's dreams come true.

When she was younger, Dalena was voted Miss Congeniality in a San Francisco beauty pageant. They chose the right person. She is always smiling. She is always happy. Dalena surrounds herself in a luminous cloak of enthusiasm. You simply cannot help but buy into what she is telling you. Dale Carnegie, the author of *How to Win Friends and Influence People,* could have learned a thing or two from Dalena. It is wonderful to be around her. It is primarily because she is enthusiastic.

One of my favorite authors who embodied enthusiasm was Dr. Norman Vincent Peale. He said, "Enthusiasm spells the difference between mediocrity and accomplishment." He wrote forty books. His most popular book, *The Power of Positive Thinking,* has sold over five million copies and has been translated into more than fifteen languages. He had a weekly radio show that ran on NBC for fifty-four years!

Dr. Peale had a heart for people. During the Depression, he was on the first advisory board of 40 Plus with James Cash Penney, the founder of J. C. Penney, and Thomas Watson, the founder of IBM. Forty Plus was founded to help executives and professionals over forty years old find jobs. It still has chapters across the country. Dr. Peale understood that helping people support themselves was a key to their happiness.

He died at the ripe old age of ninety-five. At the time of his death, he was still president of the board and chief fundraiser for an institute he started in 1954. *Guideposts* magazine, which he started with his wife, Ruth, in 1945, is not only still in circulation, but also is received by over four million households. Although he died in 1993, his work still continues to this day. His books are still read throughout the world. He has left a legacy of enthusiasm, positivism, and optimism paralleled by few.

There are many more successful people that I could include in this chapter on enthusiasm. When looking for role models, look to the enthusiastic. If you embrace this core principal of success, you will be greatly rewarded with happiness.

CHAPTER 23

POSITIVE PSYCHOLOGY

*The greatest discovery of my generation
is that human beings can alter their lives
by altering their attitudes of mind.*
—WILLIAM JAMES

Psychology started out with behaviorism. Basically, organisms re-act to a stimulus and both reaction and stimulus is measured and compared. Behaviorists study behavior with no consideration of internal mental states. Pavlov and B. F. Skinner are among the most famous behaviorists.

Sigmund Freud, born in 1856, changed psychology forever. He is considered the father of psychoanalysis, which is the verbal treatment of a patient with a psychopathology. He created the terms libido, free association, and transference.

Humanism came about with Abraham Maslow and others in the 1950s. They questioned the negative focus of psychology. Maslow is best known for his "hierarchy of needs." He explained this hierarchy in his 1954 book, *Motivation and Personality*. The needs include in ascending order: physiological, safety, love/belonging, esteem, and self -actualization.

Physiological needs include air, food, water, and sleep. Safety needs include security of the body, job, family, and property. Love/

belonging needs include friendship, family, and intimacy. Esteem needs include self-esteem, confidence, achievement, respect of others, and respect by others. Self-actualization needs include morality, creativity, spontaneity, and problem solving.

Maslow studied and focused on what he called "exemplary people," such as Eleanor Roosevelt, Einstein, and Jane Adams. He is attributed with saying, "The study of crippled, stunted, immature, and unhealthy specimens can yield only a cripple psychology and a cripple philosophy."

Maslow also invented the term "metamotivation." Metamotivated people strive for constant betterment. They are not just focused on basic human needs. Be a metamotivated person. You get one shot at life. Make the most of it. Have no regrets when it comes to effort.

There is a more recent branch of psychology, called "positive psychology." One of its founders is Martin Seligman. He was the president of the American Psychological Association in 1998. Positive psychologists seek to make life more fulfilling and not simply treat mental illness. Positive psychology complements and does not replace traditional psychology methods. It focuses on how life can be better, and how people can be happier. Boy, do we need this!

Seligman often uses the term "flourishing" in relation to human happiness. Flourishing can be defined as growing and thriving in a positive sense throughout life. To define flourishing, he created the acronym PERMA. PERMA stands for: **P**ositive emotion, **E**ngagement, **R**elationships, **M**eaning, and **A**ccomplishment

This is a branch of psychology I identify with. I wish I could have taken Dr. Laura Delizonna's course on happiness when I was getting my degree in psychology. I could not identify with all of the abnormalities that can occur in the human psyche. Luckily, I had no reference point when it came to schizophrenia. Almost all of what I studied focused on how messed up humans are.

I am a happy, optimistic person. I would rather focus on what is right instead of what is wrong. I am always searching for tips and strategies to make life better. I love to learn about any topic. I am always seeking ways to maximize my time, get there sooner, have a better meal, and be a better spouse and parent. I have great respect for this new group of psychologists.

I took Dr. Laura Delizonna's course on happiness at Stanford. She taught the course with Ted Anstedt. They are both brilliant and incredible people. In the course, we had to fill out the General Happiness Scale devised by Sonya Lyubomirsky, PhD, an associate professor of psychology at the University of California at Riverside and author of *The How of Happiness*. The scale consists of a four-question quiz. After answering the question, you add up your score and divide by four. An unhappy person would score a 1. A very happy person would score a 7. The mean for adult Americans is 4.8. I scored a 7. My fears were confirmed. I'm incredibly happy!

Professor Edward Diener, PhD at the University of Illinois is a pioneer in the study of happiness. He was told in the 1970s that you couldn't measure happiness. He disagreed, because they were measuring depression. If you can measure depression, why can't you measure happiness? He believes that happiness is a skill. I agree with him. I believe that happiness is a skill that you continually need to refine. Like a knife that needs to be sharpened regularly, you have to be vigilant to protect your happiness. You have to learn and implement new ways of becoming and continuing to be happy.

CHAPTER 24

FORGIVENESS

The weak can never forgive. Forgiveness
is the attribute of the strong.
—GANDHI

You cannot create a positive future by holding onto a negative past. You cannot have a healthy personal relationship with yourself or others without forgiveness. Forgiveness is the salve that heals hearts. Forgiveness breaks the chains to hurt and indignation. It puts out the fires of torment.

My friend, Dr. Fred Luskin teaches a famous course at Stanford on happiness. His students are lucky to have him as a teacher. He is a genius and he's hysterically funny. His course is one of the hardest courses to get into at Stanford. He is at the vanguard of positive psychology. He is best known for his work on forgiveness and stress. He is the author of *Stress Free for Good*, *Forgive for Good*, and *Forgive for Love*. He offers lectures, seminars, and trainings around the world on the importance, health benefits, and training of forgiveness, stress management, and emotional competence. Major companies have hired him to educate their employees about stress.

Dr. Luskin has a killer line on happiness. He said to me over lunch one day, "Happiness is wanting what you have. Stress is wanting something else." So learn to love what you have and don't give in to discontent. I think this is especially true when it comes to your spouse. The grass is never greener.

What is important to remember is that the past is gone. The past is ashes, no longer material or present. What we are left with are memories and emotional feelings of the past, both positive and negative. Don't let these negative feelings control your present emotions. We all have negative past experiences. We have all been hurt, harmed, harangued, and wronged. We must forgive those who have harmed us. Not for them, but for us. We must throw out our emotional junk and start with a clean slate every day. That way our thoughts and our lives will flourish in the clean, fertile, soil of our minds. Forgive!

CHAPTER 25

IT'S NOT WHERE YOU START, IT'S WHERE YOU FINISH

Everything works out in the end. And if it hasn't worked out yet, then it's not the end.
—TRACY MCMILLAN

Throughout this book I have used examples of ordinary people that came from humble beginnings and went on to change and inspire the world. Wouldn't you like to do the same? On your deathbed, wouldn't you like to look back and smile with happiness that you gave life your all?

I love stories of ordinary people that did extraordinary things, people from humble beginnings that rose to the top and inspired generations. This chapter will deal exclusively with that theme. In this book, I have listed personality traits that can manifest happiness, such as enthusiasm, forgiveness, generosity, and fearlessness. The people that I will write about in this chapter had these powerful traits.

Abraham Lincoln came from a very poor family. But why don't I let him tell his story? He wrote, "I was born Feb. 12, 1809, in Hardin County, Kentucky. My parents were both born in Virginia, of undistinguished families—second families, perhaps I should say.

My mother, who died in my tenth year, was of a family of the name of Hanks....My father...removed from Kentucky to...Indiana, in my eighth year....It was a wild region, with many bears and other wild animals still in the woods. There I grew up....Of course when I came of age I did not know much. Still somehow, I could read, write, and cipher...but that was all."

Abraham Lincoln had many setbacks. He bought a general store that failed. He ran for the Illinois General Assembly and lost. He was elected to the U.S. House of Representatives for one term and lost his reelection. He ran twice for Senate for the state of Illinois and failed. He tried to get the nomination for vice president and failed. He became the butt of many jokes and cruel cartoons. He bore the horrific burden of watching two of his sons die. He would not stop, however. He would not give in to failure. On November 6, 1860, he became the sixteenth president of the United States.

Abraham Lincoln went on to become one of the greatest presidents in the history of the country. He freed the slaves. He saved our union. He had many obstacles in his life, but he never let them stop him. His law partner said, "His ambition was a little engine that knew no rest." Try to mimic the resilience of Lincoln. Do not ever give in to your critics.

Whenever I get challenged on my line "Whatever you see in the future, you will be in the future," I think about Merlin Olsen. He was one of the Fearsome Foursome of the Los Angeles Rams. The Fearsome Foursome was considered one of the greatest defensive lines in the history of the NFL.

During his Hall of Fame Speech in 1982, Merlin Olsen described how his dream was to become an athlete. He had wanted to be an athlete since before he could remember. His high school coach cut him from the ninth-grade basketball team. The coach told him that he would never be an athlete and to let it go. He refused. He saw himself as an athlete and he became one of the best athletes of all time.

The Rams drafted him third overall in the 1962 NFL draft. He went to the Pro Bowl his rookie year. He went to an amazing fourteen straight Pro Bowls. He played for fifteen years with the Rams and had ninety-four sacks as a defensive lineman. In 1974, Olsen was voted the NFL MVP.

Merlin Olsen mentored many people in his life. Fellow Hall of Famer and teammate Jack Youngblood remembers Merlin telling him as a young player "to push to be great not just on every play, but with every heartbeat." Merlin did that on and off the field.

He parlayed his football success into acting. He was on the TV show *Little House on the Prairie* and starred in the show *Father Murphy*. He had a long sports broadcasting career. He earned a master's degree in economics while playing for the Rams. He raised a lot of money for charities, including the Children's Miracle Broadcast Network. He would work autograph shows and participate in golf tournaments and send the money to his old teammate Lamar Lundy, who was chronically ill and had no health insurance.

The famous sports broadcaster Dick Enberg said, "Socrates must have had him in mind or the Greeks did because he was the sound mind in the sound body. God doesn't create people perfectly, but he came real close with Merlin Olsen. In the history of football, if you are going to vote for the best defensive tackle in football, you've got to consider Merlin Olsen."

Olsen raised a great family and was faithful to his wife of forty-six years. He was serious about being good. How many people do you know have taken the time to sit down and write a personal mission statement? Merlin did. His mission statement for his life was, "The focus of my life begins at home with family, loved ones and friends.

I want to use my resources to create a secure environment that fosters love, learning, laughter and mutual success. I will protect and value integrity. I will admit and quickly correct my mistakes. I will be a self-starter. I will be a caring person. I will be a good listener with an open mind. I will continue to grow and learn. I will facilitate and celebrate the success of others." This mission statement is on a plaque at the base of his twelve-foot-high bronze statue, outside of Merlin Olsen Field, at his alma mater, Utah State. Not bad for a guy who was told by a trusted coach that he would never be an athlete.

CHAPTER 26

50 STEPS TO A LIFETIME OF HAPPINESS

Each step you take reveals a new horizon. You have taken
the first step today. Now, I challenge you to take another.
—DAN POYNTER

You have incredible power down deep inside of you. You have what can only be described as a raging river of untapped potential, just waiting for you to unleash it. There is an unopened door in your life that is just waiting to be opened. Reach out and turn the handle. Push the door open into your new life, your better life. Step happily over the threshold of doubt and into the light of the new you. No one else can do this for you. It is your time. In this moment, make the decision for self-mastery. Step forward and, like David, slay your Goliath of fear. Claim your victory. Show people that they were wrong about you—you won't be written off that easily. Your next act will be your best act. This triumph over opposition is your legacy. Forget turning the handle, I want you to kick that door down! Seize your destiny today and take your first step on the path to happiness.

Write this down: If we knew the precise outcomes of our behaviors, we would make the appropriate decision each and every time.

What I mean by that is: Imagine that everything you picked up to eat had a tiny TV monitor on it. A potato chip could show you what you would look like as a result of eating it. If you could see yourself getting fatter, you would put it back! If you picked up a strawberry and it showed a visual image of you in a time-lapsed fashion getting slimmer as a result of eating the strawberry, you would buy more. That is what futurizing is all about

If a smoker could pick up a pack of cigarettes and it showed them in a cancer ward with tubes in their nose and their family crying by their side at their moment of death, how many people would put down that pack?

Bill Keane authored the long-running newspaper comic *The Family Circus*. It began its run in 1960 and continues today in syndication in hundreds of papers around the country. He is credited with the saying "Yesterday is history, tomorrow is a mystery, today is a gift of God, which is why we call it the present." Change your mindset to understand that you are living a gift. You have received the present of life. It will never be perfect. It doesn't have to be, in order for you to be happy. Appreciate these precious moments and make the most of them.

I boiled down thirty years of my research on happiness into the following 50 Steps. Use this condensed version as a reference guide. When you are feeling down or need some inspiration, come back to this chapter.

50 Steps to a Lifetime of Happiness

1. **Choose to be happy.** Throughout each day, you can be happy or you can be choose from a panoply of other emotions. Choose happiness each time.
2. **Tell everyone that you care about, how much you love and deeply appreciate them.** Get detailed in your description.

Let them know what a great and positive influence they have been on your life. Take some time to write down a few key phrases and times that they have come through for you.

3. **Find your purpose.** People with a purpose are people on a mission, a happy mission. Make sure your purpose includes serving others. We all have good inside of us. When we help others with noble intentions, that good starts to spread. Joy will follow and joy will spread.

4. **Keep learning.** Take a continuing education course. Get a designation at work. Hire a life coach. The more you know, the happier you will be.

5. **Make a list of whom and what makes you happy.** Spend more time around those that make you laugh and are positive people. Do the things you love with the people you love.

6. **Find a mentor.** Find people that have "been there, done that" and are successful at it. They can shave years off of you trying to achieve your goals. Most people who have made it love to help others to the same level.

7. **Be a mentor.** It is very fulfilling to help people arrive at the right destination. Older folks generally need help with computers. When you show them tips like "Control S" or help them get on Facebook, they have such an immediate reaction of joy. That will make your day better. Younger people need wise counsel when it comes to careers and love. Be the person that you wish you always had access to when you were younger. When you are older, maybe they will help you with your computer or antigravity boot questions.

8. **Think positive.** You cannot achieve a goal that you do not believe is doable. There would be no United States without George Washington's positive thoughts that he could

overthrow British rule. He gambled all for his belief in a better life. You cannot be happy if you live a life of fear.

9. **Be grateful.** When you wake up in the morning, your first thought should be "Thank You!" Treasure the small things, like each sip of hot tea or a meal made by someone you love. The more you pay attention to gratitude, the more you realize just how good you've got it.

10. **Stop feeling sorry for yourself.** Want to drive everyone away from you? Show them how sorry you feel for yourself. Outside of your family, no one really cares. I am not saying that nobody has empathy for your situation. I am saying that people avoid people who are consistently wallowing in self-pity. When you throw a pity party, the only person that shows up is you. Table for one lonely, loser, please! Remember, you are alive. There will come a time when you won't be. You have to make the best of what you have. There is no other choice. You can be happy or you can be sad. If you choose to be happy consistently, here comes the party: friends, wealth, good times, joy, and love. If you choose to be sad consistently, here come these guys: drugs, overeating, poverty, disease, loneliness, depression, and early death. I don't know about you, but I love the party.

11. **Enjoy and celebrate your uniqueness.** You are a precious commodity. There is only one of you. Stop trying to be everyone else and accept yourself. Not everyone will like you. The people that do like you are your real friends.

12. **Prioritize your tasks.** Make a list of what you have to do every day. Assign numbers to each task. The numbers will order the most important to the least important. Do the most important things first. It is freeing to organize your day.

13. **See the silver lining.** When you are going through a rough spot, it is hard to be excited about what good could come out of it. There is always something to learn from every experience, good and bad. Try to see the good.

14. **Be kind.** Use the acronym KLAP, which stands for Kindness, Love, And Patience, when you are speaking to someone. Mean words not only hurt the other person, they will come back to hurt you in the future. People avoid impatient people. Have a reputation of kindness and you will always be welcomed wherever you go.

15. **Forgive others and yourself.** Life is too short to hold grudges. Overlook the shortcomings of others. Give people a second chance. Harboring resentment only hurts you. You will never be without fault. Move on from your shortcomings and pledge to be better in the future.

16. **Take care of your body.** Your body is your temple. If you are abusing it, you can't achieve true happiness. You must love yourself. Overeating, doing drugs, drinking too much, and not getting enough sleep will stall your true growth as a person. The mind-body connection cannot be overlooked when it comes to happiness.

17. **Set the right goals.** Noble goals, like serving and helping others, will lead to happiness. Change the world one person at a time. Be a force for good. Build a reputation as an honorable, loving person.

18. **Be a better parent.** Be gentler and more patient with your children. Just when you think you cannot take any more questions about clouds and the sky, think of the acronym KLAP (kindness, love, and patience). Read to them more. Einstein said, "If you want your children to be intelligent,

read them fairy tales. If you want them to be more intelligent, read them more fairy tales." Be the parent that you always wanted your parent to be.

19. **Be a better child.** No matter how bad or good your parents were to you, be better to them. Without them, you would not be here. Most parents tried their best. Don't carry grudges against your parents. Forgive them for their shortcomings. It will set you free. You will also set a great example for your children on how to take care of their parents. Do you see yet how goodness is a circle?

20. **Read.** What are you passionate about? There are books, websites, and countless articles written about everything. Research your passions and interests. By reading, you will discover new, tangential interests. These interests will take you in a different direction and keep you constantly engaged and interested in life.

21. **Watch Less TV.** They say that sitting is the new smoking. How many hours a day are you spending in front of the television? Try to limit your viewing hours and get out and experience life!

22. **Strengthen your faith.** Studies have shown that people of faith are generally happier people. You also have the opportunity to share fellowship with people with similar views about life. All of us are composed of three parts: mind, body, and spirit. Nourish your spirit. Pray.

23. **Schedule fun.** If you are married, have a regular date night. If you have kids, have a family night or afternoon just devoted to fun. Life can be very busy. Do not surrender your precious life to the TV.

24. **Shake off the negative.** Hurt, anger, resentment, and regret are anchors that hold us back from our divine fate. Your true

spirit yearns to soar and be free. Do not let these negative emotions nest in your soul. Shake them off and be free from the pain. They do not belong as a part of you. Refuse to be pulled down into the morass of depression. Use humor as a shield.

25. **Take action.** Do not sit there wishing a problem would go away. Make a decision to change the situation. Do whatever it takes to shake you out of that physical, mental, or financial rut.

26. **Watch what you watch.** Don't watch sad movies. When you walk out of a movie theater after watching a sad movie, do you feel great, inspired, and ready to take on life's challenges? Of course not. Watch more feel-good movies. Whatever you feed your mind will manifest itself in your life. Same thing goes for depressing music.

27. **Get out of your comfort zone.** Try new things. Run a marathon or a 5k. Go to www.meetup.com and attend a local meeting that interests you. Start crossing off items on your bucket list. Don't have a bucket list? Make one.

28. **Exercise.** Exercise boosts energy, improves mood, controls weight, combats disease, and promotes better sleep. The benefits of exercise will be a positive force in your life.

29. **Be confident.** You are an incredible creation. Self-confidence attracts people to you. It helps you make good decisions. It gets you out of analysis-paralysis. Confidence belies a sense of ease and self-acceptance. You will have more fun, be heard more, get more done, and have less fear.

30. **Travel.** Go have a glass of real champagne with a loved one while looking at the Eiffel Tower. Have a family reunion at Disneyland. Camp at a national park. See your favorite band or sports team in a different city. Whatever you have been dreaming of, it is time to do it.

31. **Laugh more.** Go see a great comedian at a local comedy club. Watch more comedies on TV and at the movies. If you have satellite radio, they have channels devoted entirely to comedy. You can actually have a good belly laugh sitting in a traffic jam. Laughter releases endorphins and helps reduce stress hormones. It also strengthens your immune system.

32. **De-clutter.** Having a clean, well-organized living environment is great for positive mental health. Give things you don't need to charity.

33. **Get a good night's sleep.** You can't take on the world if you are yawning at your desk. Use blackout shades in your room if the sun wakes you every morning before the alarm clock does.

34. **Memorize two great jokes.** If you don't have a good memory, put them on your smartphone. Jokes are a great icebreaker when you meet new people. They can also be used to lighten a tense situation. Why two jokes? The first joke is a warm-up. When everyone is laughing, you can raise the fun in the room with the second. Keep it clean and inoffensive.

35. **Come up with a great idea.** Think about ways to improve humanity. It could be an invention, a service, or a way to make an existing process better. Once you have that idea in mind, do something about it. I know someone who works with inventors. He said the worst thing you can do is keep your inventions to yourself. This idea could become your purpose and inspire you to get out of bed every morning and have a successful day.

36. **Compliment people often.** Encouragement is the invisible energy that helps drive people forward and higher. Kind words can change a person's day for the better, and could

also change their life. I remember some compliments that people gave me years ago.

37. **Smile.** Smiling is contagious. Want people to like you more? Want to make a great first impression? Smiling is the most powerful, life-changing social grace we were given.

38. **Use your vacation days at work.** You need time to rest and regroup. You will be a better worker, parent, and person when you are revitalized.

39. **Seek out social events.** Go to parties. Join an organization that helps serve others. Network with people to help build your career and social life. Humans need interaction to be happy. That is why in prison there is the threat of solitary as punishment. For as bad as prison is, solitary is worse.

40. **Give.** It doesn't matter if you don't have a lot of money. You can give your time. Give sincere compliments to people daily. Understand that as you are giving, you are gaining. You are contributing to the betterment of the universe.

41. **Ask yourself great questions.** Instead of asking yourself what would be the most decadent thing to eat when you are at a restaurant, ask yourself what would be the healthiest thing to eat that will keep you energized and fully engaged. When confronted with a choice, ask yourself if your decision will get you closer to your goal or push you further away. Instead of asking yourself "Can I?" ask yourself, "How can I?"

42. **Take pride in your appearance.** Shower every day. Wear clean clothes. When you dress your best, you feel good about yourself. It helps your self-confidence when you look good. Nobody respects a slob. As you are being wheeled into an operating room, would you trust a surgeon wearing ripped jean shorts and a dirty Iron Maiden T-shirt?

43. **Meditate.** Meditation can help provide a sense of peace. It helps to reboot your brain. It reduces stress. It helps relax the mind. It can restore order to the craziness of modern life. It can be done in as little as three minutes.

44. **Start an Up Cycle.** There is always room for improvement. Choose behaviors like eating right or exercising. An Up Cycle will be like a seed that grows and blesses you and others in your life in a positive way.

45. **Futurize.** Look out into the future. See a life at your perfect weight, a great career, and a feeling of bliss. If you can't see it, you'll never be it. Believe these feelings and they will manifest.

46. **Find a balance between work and life.** It is important not to get burned out at work. You must carve out time for your family and yourself.

47. **Stop texting and start talking to friends.** Texting is convenient and has its place. People, however, need to share their stories in detail. Having a great experience is only half the fun. Positive experiences get fully enjoyed during verbal conversation, not a one-sentence blurb on Facebook or twitter.

48. **Find the right career.** There are terrible jobs out there. Don't work in them. Believe that there is a perfect career just waiting for you to find it. Align your goals and talents with what you do. See a career counselor or read a book on careers to give you ideas on what is right for you. Talk to people in that field to find out the pros and cons. Work can be a joy or a burden. If you find your dream career, you will never want to retire.

49. **Let it go!** Don't let disappointment ruin your day. When something occurs that is not to your benefit, move on and

do the best you can going forward. Understand that set-backs happen to everyone. Great people are those most adept at not letting setbacks keep them down or dismayed.

50. **Be open to love.** My father, Michael J. Duffy, wrote, "Love is the center point of living." Love is why we are here. Loving others is great karma. What you send out, you will receive back many times over. Leave a legacy of love. Don't waste your time on this earth worried about getting your little heart broken. Be bold and accept the fact that you will get hurt from time to time. You will also be greatly rewarded. Love all races, faiths, and people. We are all God's children. Love deeply, bravely, and profoundly.

Life is a series of hurdles and challenges. As soon as you clear one hurdle, another one appears. Jump over those hurdles with deter-mination and joy. Be happy that you have this day to live. One day you won't. Look forward to the challenges and expect that this cur-rent challenge will propel you into a better future, with more friends, more success, and more opportunity. It is with age that you see that all your worries, concern, and depression were a waste of your time.

You cannot worry a problem away. You have to attack it with re-solve and expectancy. Imagine yourself like Superman with a smile and a great attitude. You are an indestructible, unstoppable, ca-pable being. When things get bad, you get badder. You are able to smash through walls and fly through the air—no one or no problem can hold you down. Commit yourself to building, learning, making progress, and helping people all around you. Make the most of this precious gift of life. Be happy. You'll be glad you did!

PART II

TAKE ACTION!

CHAPTER 27

THE HAPPINESS BOOK ACTION PLAN

*Action may not always bring happiness; but
there is no happiness without action.*
—BENJAMIN DISRAELI

Now that you have read *The Happiness Book*, it's time to take action! This chapter will help you reach your goals. Please do yourself a favor and act on your dreams. With a deadline, dreams become goals. I wish you all the best in becoming the person that you were meant to be! You can do this!

Happiness Goals
The purpose of my life is:

1

2

3

4

I will make progress toward my purpose in the following ways:

1

2

3

4

I have always wanted to travel to the following destinations:

1

2

3

4

I will have traveled to these destinations by_____ (date).

I have always dreamed of:

1

2

3

4

5

6

I will make these dreams come true by_____ (date).

I will take the following steps to make these dreams come true:

1

2

3

4

5

6

I will ask my children what their dreams are by_____ (date).

List your children's dreams here:

1

2

3

4

The following are the steps I will take to help make their dreams come true:

1

2

3

4

I will reflect on the blessings of my life _____ times per day.

I will tell everyone I love how much they mean to me by_____ (date).

The people I will contact first are:

1 Myself	7
2	8
3	9
4	10
5	11
6	12

I will pray/meditate _____ times a week.

I will forgive the following people:

1 Myself   7

2   8

3   9

4   10

5   11

6   12

I will volunteer at _____ by _____ (date).

I will give $_____ to the following charity_____ by_____
(date).

I will compliment _____ people every day.

I will read the following inspirational books in the next _____ months:

1

2

3

4

I will de-clutter my living or workspace by_____ (date).

I will get _____ hours of sleep per night.

Here are my two favorite, clean jokes:

1

2

My great idea to change the world for the better is
_____.

I will implement this idea by_____ (date).

Here are the steps in order to have this great idea come to fruition:

1

2

3

4

I will have _____ date nights per month with my significant other.

If I am single, I will find love by_____ (date).

I will employ the following steps to find this wonderful person:

1

2

3

4

I will always choose to be happy.

_____
(your signature)

Bibliography

Dyer, Wayne. *Wishes Fulfilled: Mastering the Art of Manifesting*. Carlsbad, CA: Hay House, 2012.

Dyer, Wayne, "What's My Life Purpose?". *Heal Your Life.com*, April 28, 2013. Available at http://www.healyourlife.com/author-dr-wayne-w-dyer/2013/04/wisdom/inspiration/whats-my-life-purpose

Edgar, Julie. "Types of Teas and Their Health Benefits". *WebMD*, Available at http://www.webmd.com/diet/features/tea-types-and-their-health-benefits

Hill, Napoleon. *Think and Grow Rich*. Napoleon Hill Foundation, 2012.

Luskin, Fred. *Forgive for Good*. HarperOne, 2003.

Martin, Sami K. "Tom Sullivan: 'I've Never Seen an Ugly Person Unless They Wanted to Be' Author Says His Blindness is a Blessing." *Christian Post,* October 15, 2012. Available at http://global.christianpost.com/news/tom-sullivan-ive-never-seen-an-ugly-person-unless-they-wanted-to-be-82779/#oABKyvzzk89gOoVo.99

Petit, Philippe. *Man on Wire*. Skyhorse Publishing, 2008.

Petit, Philippe. "The Journey across the High Wire." TED talk, posted May 2012. http://www.ted.com/talks/philippe_petit_the_journey_across_the_high_wire.html

Petit, Philippe. *To Reach the Clouds: My High Wire Walk Between the Twin Towers.* North Point Press, 2002.

Robbins, Anthony. *Unlimited Power: The New Science of Personal Achievement.* Pocket Books, 2001.

Seligman, Martin. *Flourish: A Visionary New Understanding of Happiness and Well-being.* Free Press, 2011.

Shenk, Joshua Wolf. "What Makes Us Happy?" *Atlantic,* June 1, 2009. http://www.theatlantic.com/magazine/archive/2009/06/what-makes-us-happy/307439

Tahir, Tariq. "Exercise and travelling top list of biggest regrets." *Metro,* November 22, 2012. Available at http://metro.co.uk/2012/11/22/exercise-and-travelling-top-list-of-biggest-regrets-540848

DISCLAIMER

The information in this book is solely for informational purposes. It is not intended to provide medical advice. Neither the author nor publisher take responsibility for any possible consequences from any treatment, procedure, exercise, lifestyle change, vacation, dietary modification, action, or application of medication that results from reading or following the information contained in this book. The author is not a physician. The publication of this information does not constitute the practice of medicine, and this information does not replace the advice of your physician or other health care provider. Before undertaking any course of treatment, the reader must seek the advice of their physician or other health care provider. If you are experiencing harmful pain or thoughts, please see a licensed health care provider immediately.

No part of the information in this book may be redistributed, copied, or reproduced without prior written consent of the author and Happiness Publishing.

Notes

Notes

Notes